The Doors We Open

Pamela Squire

The Doors We Open

by Pam Squire

Print ISBN: 978-0-578-89717-2

Copyright © 2021 by Pam Squire. All rights reserved.

Formatted for publication by Ben Wolf

www.benwolf.com/editing-services/

Printed in the United States by Believer's Book Services

www.believersbookservices.com

ENDORSEMENTS

I have known Pam for almost 30 years and the one thing I have known is that Pam is pure in her thinking and always careful what she speaks. She watches the words of her mouth. I can definitely say that Pam has expressed herself in sincerity and truth as she has experienced and studies God's Word. There is nothing like experiencing situations of deliverance and inner healing to know the truth.

Pam has major experiences in her walk. She has pastored churches, raised up and taught the people of the church how to worship God, by being a worshiper herself and knowing how to enter in. Pam is an excellent teacher of the word. She is excellent with instructing people how to grow up in Christ Jesus. You can trust Pam.

This book is much needed. And the timing is right as we will see a major need for revelation, deliverance and inner healing as we walk, which I believe, both are necessary. The times are full of darkness and Pam shines the light of Jesus Christ into situations. This book has been edited and read by several well-known ministers and we all agree this book is a must.

Jean Krisle-Blasi
Kingdom Craftsman Ministries Dallas Texas
https://www.kingdomcraftman.org

CONTENTS

1. The Beginning   1
2. Heaven   5
3. Angels   7
4. Fall Of Lucifer   10
5. Fallen Angels   15
6. Can Christians Have Demons?   17
7. How Can Demons Gain Entrance?   20
8. The Doors We Open   23
9. What Is Deliverance?   70

   About the Author   93

To my husband Jim, who is my best friend beyond Jesus. You love me as I am, believe in me, and cherish me. Thank you for who you are. To my 4 children and 17 beautiful grandchildren whom I love so very much.

Much love and thanks to Jean Krisle-Blasi, a well-known Prophet who has traveled all over the world. She has loved and mentored me and has been a Mom in the Spirit to me for near 30 years. So much wisdom and love, and balance in God.

Much love and thanks to John Sandford who now is in Heaven. A Prophet/Teacher who founded Elijah House Ministries and written many books. Thank you, Papa John, for taking my husband and I under your wing. Helping me to edit this book and mentoring us with what you learned from God over your years.

Chapter One

THE BEGINNING

In the early 1980's I was leading a bible study for women. We all decided to have time away together. An older 2 story home was located on the Oregon coast. There were approximately 15 women. The worship leader and I kept getting the same scripture "This kind come out with prayer and fasting" - Matthew 17:21, regarding this retreat. Neither of us could totally understand what this was meaning, but we knew we needed to pray and fast before the retreat. The first night around 2:00 a.m. one of the women came rushing in where some of us were sleeping and explained something terrible was happening. I quickly got up and followed. In one of the other rooms on the first floor was a woman who was huddled with her arms around herself growling and seething. I was in shock. I instinctively knew this was demonic. I started praying in my prayer language, as I knew not what to do. As I did this somehow the demon in her levitated her and she went flying across the room and hit the opposite wall and fell to the floor. I was in shock with my mouth open. The women who were in the room quickly evacuated and I was there by myself. I remember not being scared but confused in what to do. So, I continued praying. The demon in her yelled, "Stop that, or I will kill her". It was not her voice, but a deep growly masculine voice.

So, I stopped praying out loud, but then started praying in my head. It again said in the deep growly voice, "I said, stop that". The demon knew I was praying in my spiritual language. I did not know how to pray so I knew my spiritual language was what I needed to do. I knew the demon could not understand what my spirit was communicating to God. This made the demon incredibly angry. Our prayer language is a powerful tool.

When our spirit communicates with the Most Holy of Holies it empowers God in and around us. Not because of us, but because of who God is! Prayer is a powerful weapon, both type of prayers, and the enemy knew this.

All the sudden, I heard the women in the front room starting to worship. The worship leader started leading them in a song about the blood of Jesus. The demon in this woman went totally crazy. I heard the Holy Spirit say, "Speak and pray the Blood of Jesus over her and do not stop till she becomes still." It took about 30 minutes or so and finally it broke, and she became still and quiet. She was exhausted and did not remember any of it. At that moment, I learned about how the blood of Jesus, is the most powerful tool we can use in warfare against any evil entity.

No one had experienced this before in their walk with Jesus. We all returned to our beds. Then about an hour later, someone came back in where I was sleeping, and said that the beds upstairs, in one of the rooms, were jumping and shaking up and down. I thought, "What! Now what do I do?" I heard the Lord say to send the spirit to His throne for judgment. It reminded me of the scripture in Jude 1:9 when the archangel Michael was disputing over the body of Moses with the devil, he said "The Lord Rebuke you." Here Michael is the angel of the Lord and does not rebuke but states "The Lord Rebuke you." I find that remarkably interesting and something to think about.

We tend to think it is our battle, when really the battle is the Lords.

We did this and all became calm and quiet again. No more problems for the rest of the retreat time.

Did the woman get free? All I know is some healing did happen, but sometimes there are layers. Instant deliverance can happen, but a lot of times we can have layers of hurts, from abuse and or trauma. It is like an onion and peeling one layer at a time. We can trust Jesus with how He decides to see healing. I believe not only did He begin healing in her, but He was training and showing each lady on this retreat, who He is. I know this lady needed much inner healing from abuse as a child and had physical ailments. I do believe and have been told that she never manifested like that again.

So began the journey I never thought I would travel.

———

As a child my favorite times were spent down by a creek running through our property. I was so free and talked to God as my friend. I did not have religion and only knew He was my best friend. My parents did not go to church, but somehow, I knew God. I told Him everything.

I remember the first time I understood that Jesus was His son. I was in the 5th grade and saw the show at the theatre King of Kings. I remember crying as Jesus was crucified. It was not till I was in the 9th grade in August of 1969, at a Church Camp that I understood that Jesus would have died for me, even if I were the only one left on the earth. He loved me that much. I remember crying and crying because of what he had done for me. From that time on He showed me who He is. My friend, my Savior, my Father, my Healer, my Provider and through an extremely hard time in my life He showed me He was my Husband.

Next few pages I will be discussing Heaven, Angels, the fall of Lucifer and some or the Angels. I want to lay a foundation of what will be shared in this book. I will be sharing what I feel is needed throughout this book to understand how we invite darkness into our lives. Times have so changed and we are living in a time where the enemy has not stayed hidden but has revealed himself more than ever. There is a lot deeper study into what I will be sharing and will leave that up to the reader. I pray the information I give will allow each reader to seek God on what He says about things in their lives, to save them from all the hardship that these open doors can let in.

Chapter Two

HEAVEN

We know from scripture some things about Heaven. We always talk about Heaven being up. Scripture talks about the 3 heavens – 2 Corinthians 12:2. Some believe they are layers or even side dimensions. Whether up or side by side dimensions, no one knows, but here are facts that we do know from scripture.

- Heaven is joyful   Psalm 16:11
- Heaven is beautiful – Psalm 50:2
- Heaven is a place of unity - Ephesians 1:10
- Heaven has no night – Rev 21:25; 22:5
- Heaven has singing – Isaiah 44:23; Rev 14:3, 15:3
- Heaven has learning – I Corinthians 13:9-10
- Heaven has serving – Rev 7:15, 22:3
- Heaven is a place of Holiness – Rev 22:1
- Heaven has a glorious city – Rev 21:11, 18
- The Throne of God sits in its center – Rev 4:2, 22:1
- Heaven shines with and is lighted by God's Glory – Rev: 21:11
- Heaven's gates will never be shut – Rev: 21:25
- Heaven is being prepared for us by Christ – John 14:3

- Heaven is for those who are born again – John 3:3
- Heaven is a place for all eternity – John 3:15, Psalms 23:6
- Gods' angels reside in Heaven – Mark 12:25

Chapter Three

ANGELS

We do not know when angels were created, but they already existed when God created the earth. They are created beings, created by God, but they are not human - Ps. 103: 20-21, Psalm 148:2-5. We do know they reside in Heaven -Mark 12:25.

We do not know how many there are. Scripture tells us there is no increase or decrease in angels, and they do not die - Luke 20:36, Luke 2:13, Daniel 7:10, Matthew 18:10.

The Hebrew word for angel is "malakh" and the Greek word is "angelos". Both words translate to "messenger". They can become human messengers, or supernatural beings.

- Human messengers - 1Sam 6:21, Isaiah 44:26, Matt. 11:10, Luke 7:24, James 2:25
- Heavenly messengers– Ps. 104:4, Matt. 4:6, Luke 1:11, Rev. 16:1.
- Angels protect - Gen.19: 10-11, 2 Kings 6:15-17.
- Angels comfort – 1 Kings 19:5, Acts 27: 23-24.
- Angels deliver – Acts 5:19.
- Angels minister at death – Luke 16:22.
- Angels inform and instruct – Luke 2:9-12, Luke 1:26-23.

Angels worship – Psalm 29:1-2, Isaiah 6:3, 1Kings 22:19, Rev. 4:8, Rev. 19:4.

Angels and man are both created beings who were created to worship, love, obey and serve God. Angel's powers do not equal God's power, nor are they superior to Christ's position - Heb. 1:5-14. But their powers are greater than man's - 2Peter 2:11. God has granted the angels unusual strength - Ps.103:20, Matt 28:2. God has also allowed some elements of nature to be under their control - Rev. 7:1, 14:18. Their powers come from God and are only carried out according to God's law of nature and the spiritual world - Dan 6:22, Luke 24:2-4, Acts 12:7-10.

Angels are curious about us. They observe us - 1Cor. 4:9, 11:10, 1Tim. 5:21. and they will gain a better understanding of God's wisdom as they watch things come about through the body of Christ - Eph: 3:9-10. They want to understand redemption and they observe the affairs of Christ's church with awe - 1Peter 1:12, 1Cor.4:9, 11:10, 1Tim5:21.

They know when salvation happens in Christ and rejoice over it - Luke 15:10. They stay busy ministering to God and us and are not physical beings, although they can appear to us that way - Matt 1:20, Luke 1:26, John 20:12, Heb 1:14. They cannot be everywhere at once Dan - 9:21-24, 10:10-14.

We know angels do have emotions, can communicate intelligently and have free will. This we can see from the rebellion of Lucifer and the angels who followed him. Angels do not flaunt their powers. They appear to be shy. They want only to point to God and give Him glory and not want to draw attention to themselves.

There is no mention in the Bible that angels will rule and reign with Christ, but scripture does say we will - 2Tim 2:12, Rev. 5:10, 20:6, 22:5.

In the Old Testament, men are called servants, and the angels called sons of God, but in the New Testament man is called son of God and angels are referred as servants. Because of Christ's death on the cross, now we are seen by God, through Jesus' blood, and are in the likeness of Christ.

Heaven has order. In scripture angels in Heaven are organized and have rankings.

Common terminology is rulers, principalities, powers, thrones and dominions. Colossians 1:16 - For in him all things were created: things in heaven and on earth, visible and invisible, whether thrones, or powers or rulers or authorities. The angels that are known as authorities serve under the arch angels.

Angels that serve as arch angels have been given specific dominion and carry out

God's sovereign will. Archangel Michael is known as Chief Prince in Dan. 10:13 and

Great Prince in Dan. 12:1. He is the ruler over all the angels. Gabriel name means God is my power. Michael means who is like God. Their name points back to God and not to who they are. Angels are images of God's presence and power. We are told not to worship the angels - Col. 2:18, only God Himself.

Angels who serve at the throne have their place in the immediate presence of God. Cherubim are angels of power and majesty. They surround the throne of God and defend His Holiness from any contamination by sin - Exodus 25:18-20, Ezk 1:5-14, 28:12-14 & 17. They are to guard and have not been known to bring revelation or instruction from God to man. They are portrayed as beautiful and most powerful in the order of angels. They are not little chubby babies with wings.

Seraphim, as known in Hebrew, are God's flaming ones. Their consuming devotion is to serve God. Two of their wings cover their feet because of being on Holy Ground before God. With the other two pair of wings, they fly and carry out the commands of God from the throne and they sing out Holy, Holy - Is. 6:1-3.

Chapter Four

FALL OF LUCIFER

Ezekiel 28:11-19, Isa 14:12-17

Lucifer was the leading worshipping angel before God's throne. He became proud and wanted to be like God and thus fell into rebellion against God. He was thrown from Heaven along with 1/3 of the angels who followed him - Revelation12:7-9.

Genesis 1 - 3 talks of Adam and Eve being in the garden and of the deception which took place there. Adam and Eve decided to listen to the serpent and to eat from the tree of knowledge, of which God had said they were not to eat. Their choice to go against what God said, and to listen to what the enemy said gave the enemy the right to become the prince of this world. This disobedience in the garden affected other angels Rev - 12:7, all of mankind - Eph. 2:2 and gave Lucifer position as ruler of this world and power to affect the nations of this world - John 16:11, Rev. 20:3.

These are Lucifer's characteristics:

He can make you think he is from God, is God, or an angel of light, deceiving us so that visions we may have, or what we hear prophetically, or what we think is, is not of God.

False prophecies can be words spoken through others to us, or words we may have received from others. It is important that we do not prophesy out of our own soul or heart. Deception creates what the Bible calls false prophets, false prophecies, and deceitful workers. Just because something feels good and seems to be right does not mean it is. That is why it is important to check all things by God and His word and by what the Holy Spirit says in a situation. We need to know God and His heart. People do not realize that we can prophesy through our own flesh or understanding, through the worlds view of things, through a demonic entity, through being sensitive and reading a person's heart and what their desires are. It is so important to know who God is and it be what He is communicating. Gods' love deals with us each individually. We sometimes think everything fits in a box for everyone.

Satan used scripture against Jesus in the wilderness - Matthew 4: 1-11 - Then Jesus was led by the Spirit into the wilderness to be tempted[a] by the devil. 2 After fasting forty days and forty nights, he was hungry. 3 The tempter came to him and said, "If you are the Son of God, tell these stones to become bread." 4 Jesus answered, "It is written: 'Man shall not live on bread alone, but on every word that comes from the mouth of God.'[b]" 5 Then the devil took him to the holy city and had him stand on the highest point of the temple. 6 "If you are the Son of God," he said, "throw yourself down. For it is written: "He will command his angels concerning you, and they will lift you up in their hands, so that you will not strike your foot against a stone.'[c]" 7 Jesus answered him, "It is also written: 'Do not put the Lord your God to the test.'[d]" 8 Again, the devil took him to a very high mountain and showed him all the kingdoms of the world and their splendor. 9 "All this I will give you," he said, "if you will bow down and worship me." 10 Jesus said to him, "Away from me, Satan! For it is written: 'Worship the Lord your God and serve him only.'[e]" 11 Then the devil left him, and angels came and attended him.

Jesus' knowledge of His Father in Heaven was the key to His ability to discern. We want to be guided by God's truth and nothing else! That is why it is important we know our Father in heaven and His heart.

Satan cannot create, but he and his demons can imitate.

Exodus talks about how Aaron's rod was thrown down and it turned into a snake. Then how Pharaohs men threw down their rods and they turned into snakes. Aarons snake ate the other's snakes - Exodus 7:10-12.

Satan has usurped authority and become the god of this world, and uses various philosophies, religions, secular humanism, and cults to delude people. He is the force behind all these beliefs that are not biblical. In each of us God has created a place in our hearts that only He can fill. Satan tries to fill that area with wrong "religious" teachings so that we feel we are holy in our own fleshly doings. Satan wants us to believe that our value systems and our worldviews are acceptable to God.

Satan is the father of lies. He adds things that may seem right but are not. He uses some scriptures while leaving out other scriptures that counterbalance. He did that with Christ in the wilderness after His Baptism - Matthew 4: 1-11, John 8:42-47. He does that to the church today. We take one scripture and think we know because it fits what we want to believe.

Satan makes people think all supernatural things must be from God. He makes religion seem right and holy, but religion is not who God is. God is a God of RELATIONSHIP! It is Christ's blood that saves us, not what man's religiosity requires.

Religion is man trying to be right with God, doing things to make us look worthy to God. Jesus has already paid the ultimate price. That is why it is important to know God and not rely on man's knowledge. Man can be off in his understanding of what and who God is because we are only man. We live here on earth and do not understand the Kingdom of God. What seems fair here is not necessarily how God sees it. The Holy Spirit wants to give us His truth so that we will be in BALANCE. We can all take scripture out of context to make a point. We need to find all the scriptures on all subjects and ask God to bring it all into balance by who He is. Western man has taken a lot of scriptures out of context. It is important to know what the culture was, and what was being addressed culturally. Balance, balance, balance is so important in our walk in Christ.

Satan states he does not exist. That is the biggest lie he loves people to believe. He puts a veil over believer's eyes and blinds the eyes of non-believers - 2Cor 4:3-4. He questions if the Word of God is true. He did this in the Garden of Eden when he asked Eve, "Did God really say?" - Rev 12:9, 20:2.

He tempts believers to sin – Eph 2: 1-3, 1Thess 3:5. He tempts us to lie – Acts 5:3. He sets us up for pride to puff us up- 1Tim 3:6.

He tempts believers to commit sexual immorality – 1Cor. 7:5. He sows tares among the believers – Matt 13: 38-39. He tries to hinder the work of believers in any way he can – 1Thes. 2:18. He tricks believers into the things that are not God – 2Cor 11:3.

His primary method is to cause discord between believers. He keeps us focused on the negative, the sins and shortcomings of what is in others or ourselves, and to keep non-believers walking away from God. His goal is to destroy mankind.

In 1991 we started a church in our home. It grew fast. Our hearts were to see people set free and grow in their relationship to Jesus. We were soon in one building and had to move to another because of growth. The worship brought in the presence of the Lord. We began having the Toronto blessing before Toronto did. There was a cloud of the Lord's presence that would come in. I later understood it was His Shekinah Glory. People began to be set free, healed, and renewed. One morning we showed up to church and there was a satanic pentagram chalked at our front door.

As most Christians do, we think oh well, no problem, erase it. Satan has no power. We did not spiritually understand we needed to come together and break the power of curses over the church. Jesus does have the total authority, but the enemy uses sins of man to destroy and if there is an opening it will find its way. It became a real learning time for me.

We had Barbara and Jean who are greatly gifted and anointed, come and helped us through the time of raising this church up.

They would visit the church periodically and bring edification and God's word. I remember Barbara telling us a story of a church that God was using mightily.

She told us of a church she was ministering to in Arizona. The Satanists in the area sent in some of their people in from their coven, to destroy this work. After a time, the head Satanist, gave his life to Jesus. When Barbara asked him, what made him come to understand who Jesus was, He said the coven could not penetrate the church because of the love that was there for one another.

If it were not for Christ, we would not be here. His love was the ultimate love of laying down His life. In His sacrifice of death, He took back all the legal right the enemy has over us. But we too, must give over our lives to Him for it come into play for us.

Rev 12:11 states "They overcame him, by the blood of the Lamb and the word of their testimony. They did not love their lives so much as to shrink from death." This is a powerful part of scripture. This is how the enemy is defeated! Speaking His Blood over our lives and others is one of the most powerful tools we can use against the enemy. Coupled with the testimony we share of our walking through the trials and tribulations brought about in our lives. Making sure Christ receives all the glory, taking up the cross in our lives as He did for us, to the end. Just as Paul said, "Run the race well" - 2Timothy 4:7. Our testimony or life is never about us, but about the Lord!

Chapter Five
FALLEN ANGELS

The Bible speaks about the war that happened in heaven in which 1/3 of the angels were cast out with Lucifer, because of their rebellion. These are the fallen angels or demons. 2Peter 2:4, Jude 1:6; Rev 12:7-12.

In the Bible they are alluded to as principalities, powers, dominions, thrones, princes, lords, gods, angels of light, spirits, unclean spirits, and wicked spirits. In scripture there are different levels under Lucifer as the dominate headship. Matt 25:41, Eph. 6:12, Rev 12:7

- Demons cause jealousy and factions among believers - James 3:13-16.
- They want to separate us from Christ anyway they can - Rom 8:38-39.
- They serve and co-operate with Satan to do their deeds against man - Matt 25:41, Eph. 6:12, Rev. 12:7-12.
- In the end they will be cast into the burning flames with Satan - Luke 8:31.

There is a book by Howard Pittman who had pastored a Baptist Church and was a Police Officer. The book is called

Placebo. He shares his experience how an angel of the Lord took him to where the demons reside, and he relates what he saw. He was shown our world and saw it in the spiritual realm regarding the angels and demons and how they mingle among us, and then he was taken to Heaven. He came back from death to share what he saw. He talks about being in 3 places: The realm where the demonic live, and how they can come into our realm and their place of existence. He talks about seeing our realm through the spirit, and then the place where God resides. If you go online and look the title and his name, you will also see video's you can listen to, on what he saw.

I have not myself experience what he experienced, but it was interesting reading and may help you understand the spiritual realm we live in. Just because we do not see things, does not mean it is not there.

We cannot walk a perfect life here in this present world, but there are many ways we can open doors to the enemy. We live in a world that has a spiritual realm that we cannot always understand or see. God created the Spiritual realm, but the enemy uses it. The enemy has no power to create, but he can mimic, and create illusions. We must be wise. We need to know our enemy and his plans. We need to rely on the Holy Spirit and what guidelines God gives for our protection. Yes, there is protection that God's grace and the blood of Jesus does cover, but where the line is for each of us may be different because of what we do know. No one is perfect except through the blood of Christ. God now can look at us through His sons' blood. The blood of a perfect sacrifice. We are not perfect, but we can be aware and use wisdom and balance as we walk out our lives here on earth. God made a way for us. • John 14:6 - Jesus answered, "I am the way and the truth and the life. No one comes to the Father except through me. If you really know me, you will know my Father as well.

Chapter Six

CAN CHRISTIANS HAVE DEMONS?

The Greek word for demonized is "dianonizomai". When the Greek language is spoken it transmits to its hearer a picture of what has just been said. This word itself, means degrees of influence of demons.

When I was working as a Doctor's assistant and Triage, a scale was used to ask people what their pain level was. It was numbered 1 to 10 with different faces from smiling, to sad, to tears running down the face. This is called a numeric pain distress scale that is accompanied with faces called the Wong-Baker face pictures. These faces help rate pain in the patient.

The word "dianonizomai" can look like that scale below because of the degrees a person can be demonized. Number 1 being lightly influenced and number 10 being totally possessed. This all depends on how much we have given place to the enemy in our life.

Slightly influenced				Medium		Strongly influenced			Possessed
1	2	3	4	5	6	7	8	9	10

When King James called together men of that time to translate the Cannon into the KJV, so it would be readable to the English, the Greek word Dianonizomai was mistranslated as "possession" which in our language interprets total control. Some of the scriptures were translated right, with the meaning of total control (because there was total possession), but others were not translated right, and can mean the person was under a degree of influence of demons. When we start translating from one language to another meaning of words can be lost. That is why it is so important to go back to the original language to check things out.

I worked in a Christian bookstore in the 90's, and people would come in and want only the KJV, what they stated was the only true version. What they did not understand is the Original Greek for New Testament and Hebrew for the Old is the true version. And yes, with KJV the same thing happened when they translated the wordings from the original text. They have found wrong word translations that are not correct, so additions are still being made and what they call revised.

We can be susceptible to any of the enemy's strategies to place strongholds in our lives, whether we are believers, non- believers, or atheists. The Greek word for salvation is "sotso" which translated means a continuing process that we grow in salvation daily.

I will not argue if we can or cannot lose our salvation. I am not the judge. God is. He takes each of us individually and will judge us; accordingly, Jesus judging the believers and God Himself judging everything else. He alone knows the heart of each of us and the path we have walked.

Because of the Satan's tactics it is important to know his strategies. His biggest lie is God does not exist and Satan does not exist.

Nothing is new under the sun - Ecclesiastics 1:9. His strategies do not change; he just has had a long time to perfect them to entangle us, so that he can destroy mankind. That is his goal.

So, the question is, "Can Christians have degrees of demonic holds?" Because of where I have walked and what I have seen, I will have to say absolutely they can. "Can Christians be totally possessed?" I would have to say no, unless they walk away, deny Christ, and start serving other things in their lives, then there is that chance. If they totally decide to become Satanist, I believe they will become fully possessed. But God still can overcome, if the person really wants set free and believes only God can save them. Repenting of our sins is the key and then learning how to forgive ourselves and others.

Chapter Seven

HOW CAN DEMONS GAIN ENTRANCE?

When we sin, and there is not with TRUE repentance, we give a legal right for Satan and his demons to have access to us. True repentance means turning 180 degrees the other way. Not just sorry for a short time and returning to the old ways. You cannot rebuke a devil that you continuously grant access to your life. When you go back to old ways, you leave a door wide open and may let more demons back in. Matthew 12:43 – 45 says - When an impure spirit comes out of a person, it goes through arid places seeking rest and does not find it. Then it says, I will return to the house I left. (It will try to regain entrance.) When it arrives, it finds the house unoccupied, swept clean and put in order. Then it goes and takes with it seven other spirits more wicked than itself, and they go in and live there. (Because the person has left doors open.) And the final condition of that person is worse than in the first.

We must remember, we step in to see someone set free if they genuinely want deliverance and we know it is ok for us to be a part of that, or we see God initiating it. We do not want to cause that person to have more demons inhabit them. God knows the perfect timing. So important to follow His timing and not our own thinking.

It is so important for us to close doors in our lives. Therefore, I feel it is so important to understand where these doors are. One of the biggest I feel is unforgiveness. Forgiving any person, we have taken an offense against. Forgiveness does not mean we forget, but we release those who have hurt or offended us. Even if we may feel we have a right to hold that offense against them. When Jesus was betrayed and He hung from the cross, He said, "Forgive them, Father, for they know not what they do" - Luke 23:34. Jesus set the path for us to follow so we can be in line with the Father. If we focus on the hurt, we will continue to suffer. If we focus on the lesson, we will continue to grow and be healed.

When we do not truly repent, forgive a person, or continue in the same sin, we have made the decision to put ourselves in a prison and chains. We then literally tie the hand of God from being able to intervene on our behalf. We wonder why nothing is changing in our life. We have tied Gods hand with our choices.

God has given us and His angel's freedom of choice. God does not want puppets, but He wants those who will love Him, serve Him, and obey Him with all their heart. He wants us choosing His way with our choices. When we repent, forgive, and turn away from sin, it gives us back our legal protection in Christ. All because of what Jesus did on that cross for us. He came as man, a man with no sin, laid His life down for each of us, so we can regain our inheritance and communion with God. God now sees us through the blood of His son. And Christ restored us to the Father in Heaven by His death.

When God created the heavens and earth, He created order and principles of righteousness. When we go against the order He created, there are consequences that come into our lives. It is not that He is out to get us, but He set His laws and motions in progress, long before we entered this world because of His love for His creation.

Sometimes we think we are ok, even if we have opened a door, because things seem to be going ok. From what I have experienced and seen, there can be a grace period that God allows before we suffer the consequences of our chosen sin, because of His love He wants us to repent. So do not think you can walk in sin because everything seems to be going okay. That is one of the biggest lies the enemy gives. Satan loves to mask the truth.

Satan will make sure everything is coming up roses, so you will continue in your ways. What goes around will come around. And it will be only a short time before Gods principles hit. Then we wonder why everything has turned upside down. We blame God, everyone, and everything, but our own choices.

It is so important to know God and His heart and to obey His ways. Obedience is better than sacrifice. That is one to really meditate on and understand. God's ways are way beyond our comprehension. What man may think, may not be how God sees it. His ways are perfect, and He sees all the twists and turns. He set up His ordnances for our protection because He loves us and wants protection for us from the fallen ones of this world.

Chapter Eight

THE DOORS WE OPEN

Occult and Witchcraft

Involvement innocently or intentionally opens a big door for demons to access power and control over someone. Because of the hold this can have, deliverance can be long and hard, especially if someone has been delving in occult and witchcraft knowingly. But God still will and can overcome this in someone's life.

I know back when Harry Potter series hit the scene, my heart just wept. We do not realize what we allow our children to be entertained by. It seems so innocent and not the dark occult. But it is all witchcraft in God's Kingdom. There is no such thing as casting spells that are good. It is all black magic and is an abomination to God. It opens things up in our lives that will bring back lash. People do not understand that Satan will want something in return when you enter his realm. He will demand pay back from you, where God gave His son Jesus as a sacrifice. He paid the price. We owe nothing but to turn our hearts and lives to God Himself. White or black, doing magic spells is all the same.

I had a friend who in her early years was into Wicca. She thought she was a good witch and blessed people with good spells. She felt she was a good witch, and those worshiping Satan were the bad witches. She mixed Christianity with her belief system. When she finally came to know the truth biblically, she asked forgiveness and her whole life changed, for she really understood the wrongness of her ways. She was a magnificent prophetic children's minister. She loved children. Her health was always an issue and she believed that dabbling in the witchcraft in her past had an effect in her present health conditions. No matter how innocent it all seems, the enemy will demand his payment for being in his realm. Yes, God wants us free and loves us, but our choices can cause circumstances that can be hard to walk free of. Health issues are not the only thing we can suffer from when being in this realm. Our disobedience can carry on down our family line generational. We can bring harm to our descendants.

We can open the wrong doors in our lives by dabbling in or using spells and Witchcraft:

- Leviticus 19:26 – Do not practice divination or seek omens.
- 1 Chronicles 10:13 – Saul died because he was unfaithful to the LORD; he did not keep the word of the LORD and even consulted a medium for guidance.
- 1 Samuel 15:23 – For rebellion is like the sin of divination, and arrogance like the evil of idolatry.
- 2 Chronicles 33:6 – He sacrificed his children in the fire in the Valley of Ben Hinnom, practiced divination and witchcraft, sought omens, and consulted mediums and spiritists. He did much evil in the eyes of the LORD, arousing God's anger.
- Leviticus 19:31 – Do not turn to mediums or seek out spiritualists, for you will be defiled by them. I am the LORD your God.
- Leviticus 20:6 – I will set my face against anyone who turns to mediums and spiritualists to prostitute themselves by following them, and I will cut them off from their people.

- Revelation 21:8 – But the cowardly, the unbelieving, the vile, the murderers, the sexually immoral, those who practice magic arts, the idolaters and all liars—they will be consigned to the fiery lake of burning sulfur. This is the second death.

- Galatians 5:19-21 – 19 The acts of the flesh are obvious: sexual immorality, impurity and debauchery; 20 idolatry and witchcraft; hatred, discord, jealousy, fits of rage, selfish ambition, dissensions, factions 21 and envy; drunkenness, orgies, and the like. I warn you, as I did before, that those who live like this will not inherit the kingdom of God.

- Micah 5:10-12 – In that day," declares the LORD, "I will destroy your horses from among you and demolish your chariots. 11 I will destroy the cities of your land and tear down all your strongholds. 12 I will destroy your witchcraft and you will no longer cast spells.

- Acts 19:17-20 – 17 When this became known to the Jews and Greeks living in Ephesus, they were all seized with fear, and the name of the Lord Jesus was held in high honor. 18 Many of those who believed now came and openly confessed what they had done. 19 A number who had practiced sorcery brought their scrolls together and burned them publicly. When they calculated the value of the scrolls, the total came to fifty thousand drachmas. 20 In this way the word of the Lord spread widely and grew in power.

- Isaiah 8:19 – When someone tells you to consult mediums and spiritualists, who whisper and mutter, should not a people inquire of their God? Why consult the dead on behalf of the living?

- Acts 8:9-13 – Now for some time a man named Simon had practiced sorcery in the city and amazed all the people of Samaria. He boasted that he was someone great, 10 and all the people, both high and low, gave him

> their attention and exclaimed, "This man is rightly
> called the Great Power of God." 11 They followed him
> because he had amazed them for a long time with his
> sorcery. 12 But when they believed Philip as he
> proclaimed the good news of the kingdom of God and
> the name of Jesus Christ, they were baptized, both men
> and women. 13 Simon himself believed and was
> baptized. And he followed Philip everywhere,
> astonished by the great signs and miracles he saw.

Just because someone may do what seems like a powerful thing or prophesies what seems to be truth, does not mean that person is doing it in the name of the Lord. They can be using sorcery. When people want power and recognition, they are not using the gifting for God, they are in the wrong realm.

- Deuteronomy 18:10-12 -Let no one be found among you
  who sacrifices their son or daughter in the fire, who
  practices divination or sorcery, interprets omens,
  engages in witchcraft, 11 or casts spells, or who is a
  medium or spiritualist or who consults the dead. 12
  Anyone who does these things is detestable to the
  LORD...

Christians can also be walking in witchcraft without being aware of it. Christians can be praying their own thinking about a situation, their own agenda in a situation thinking it is God, or praying their own thoughts, thinking they are praying Gods' will for someone. This is witchcraft. Remember, Christ takes each of us as an individual, and what is for one person may not be the route He is doing in the next individual's life. It is so important to have God's heart for someone. We tend to put everything in its own slot. But what we must understand is that not everything fits in a slot that we have created. God does not necessarily use slots. How he deals in one person's life may not be the way he does with the next. We must be so careful that we are in tune with what the Holy Spirit wants us to pray. Christians can be speaking curses into someone's life without knowing or praying something that is not what God is doing. Scripture is noticeably clear that our tongues have incredible power and can be the most difficult thing to control. We can curse or bring life with our tongues, but so important not creating something that is not God.

- Proverbs 18:21 Death and life are in the power of the tongue

Even prophesying, we can innocently speak something that is not God, even if it sounds good. The bible is specific that all may prophesy. That does not make someone a prophet, just because we prophesy. There are many voices we can hear. Our own, the enemy, the world, and God's.

- 1Corinthians 14:5 - I would like every one of you to speak in tongues, but I would rather have you prophesy. The one who prophesies is greater than the one who speaks in tongues, unless someone interprets, so that the church may be edified.
- 1Corinthians 14:31 – For you can all prophesy in turn so that everyone may be instructed and encouraged. When we gather in Christ, we all come under His spirit.

What we need to understand is that we can pick up from a persons' heart what they may be thinking or wanting to hear. Without realizing it, we end up prophesying what their heart wants, or what our heart feels, instead of what God is honestly saying. The prophets in the OT ended up doing this and God was not happy. Ezekiel 13: 1-3 Son of man, you must speak to the prophets of Israel for me. They are only saying what they want to say. You must speak to them. Tell them this: Listen to the message from the Lord. This is what the Lord God says, bad things will happen to you foolish prophets. You are following your own spirits. You are not telling people what you really see in visions. Israel, your prophets are false prophets....... This can end up being witchcraft. Some people have a gift that makes it easier to pick up people's feelings. Psychology today calls it a Highly Sensitive person. It is stated that about 20% of the population is wired this way from the womb. I call it a gifting that God gives a person. They are more intuitive than most people. We need to be aware of what we feel or hear and where it is coming from; Is it our perspective, the person's wants or feelings, the world's point of view, God's perspective, or the enemy. We want it to be God and nothing else.

It is so important to hear only the Holy Spirit! The Bible is a good source and guide to make sure we line up with God's heart and ways. Yes, we all will miss it, but both the hearer and receiver need to remember balance. If it is truly God, it will come to pass. If it does not come to pass, then we need to concentrate on God so He can create what He is doing and not give in to our own vain imaginations or our own wants and thinking. Scripture talks about having faith, as a mustard seed – Matthew 17:20-22. A mustard seed is one of the tiniest seeds. Faith is not how much you believe, but trusting in who He is, whether something comes to pass or not. He is always in control of all things.

Seeking out psychics, mediums, shamans, healers, mystical religions, witchcraft and spells of any kind:

- Leviticus 19:31 – Do not turn to mediums or seek out spiritualists, for you will be defiled by them. I am the LORD your God.
- Leviticus 20:6 – I will set my face against anyone who turns to mediums and spiritualists to prostitute themselves by following them, and I will cut them off from their people.

I believe all of us are born with gifts given by God, but we can use them in the wrong way and can be influenced by other things, instead of God. God created the spiritual realm, but again Satan and demons will use it for their purpose, too. Most prophets of the Bible heard God and used the gift given by Him for God's people.

There are words the world has given for those with gifts God has placed on them or come down through their heritage. These people are gifted but have used it from the wrong realm. Psychics, mediums, fortune tellers & others can use their gift from a wrong source. Demons can appear as an angel of light, spirit guide or whatever, and tell correct things about someone's life. Demons have been before the beginning of this world, so they know things about us, too. Demons are given assignments to people and know intimate things concerning a person. They have been around forever and have watched everything. They are highly organized and knowledgeable. The line between light and dark can be very thin in the spiritual realm and earthly realm. So, use caution and discernment whether it is man's heart talking, someone hearing a demon posing as from God. Not everything we hear or see is of God. There can also be false prophets and prophecy. Just because it is true does not mean it is from God. The bible says demons can appear as angels of light.

- 2 Corinthians 11: 14 – And no wonder, for Satan himself masquerades as an angel of light.

From the time I can remember, as a child and forward, I always talked to God. He was my best friend. I would just know things that were never told to me about people and things. I just had this knowing of things and I could feel people and their hurts. I thought everyone operated this way because it was so natural to me.

When I was in the 8th grade, I was sitting at my desk and all the sudden I just had the knowing that my mom had just been in a wreck, but I knew that she was ok.

When I got home that day from school, no one was there, which was out of the ordinary. About an hour later the secretary from my dad's work stopped by to give me the message. She knocked and I opened the door and I immediately blurted out, "My mom has had a wreck."

She looked shocked and asked, "How did you know that? Did someone tell you?"

I said, "No one told me."

She looked at me very strangely. My mom ended up being in the hospital for a week.

So, growing up, I had a gift given by God that I did not understand. People would ask me, "How did you know that?" I would just shrug my shoulders. I had no way of explaining it. I thought that was how everyone was. I slowly found out not everybody functioned this way. When a prophetic gifting is given by God to a person, the enemy knows it. The enemy will send assignments against this gift and try and take people in the opposite direction of what God intended and use the gifting in a wrong way and wrong realm. Because of this, the enemy wanted to take me in a direction, away from God's intentions. I started being drawn to things of a supernatural source. I started wondering if I had ESP. During this time, I asked my mom for a Ouija board, thinking it was just a game. Things started happening that did not feel right. I threw it away. Later years, after understanding what it was, I repented of my involvement in it. In today's world even the non-Christians will warn people about opening doors from a Ouija board. In the supernatural world this is a no-no. They too understand how dangerous this is.

In my late 20's early 30's, God was so gracious to lead me to a book by Johanna Michaelson called "The Beautiful Side of Evil". It opened my eyes to a lot of things. She had a spirit guide who said he was Jesus. She eventually wanted to know the truth about her gifting. Her grandmother had been a medium/Psychic and said it had passed down to her through the blood line. Johanna started having weird things happen and finally asked God to show her the truth with her gifting. What God did was show her that the spirit guide she was communicating with was not Jesus. God melted the outer image of this spirit guide when it reappeared. It melted like wax and underneath was an ugly demon posing as Jesus. She saw the truth and it changed her life.

Demons can appear as a spirit guide and tell truthful things. They see and hear and know about each of us. They have been around since they were thrown out of Heaven by God, because of their rebellion against Him.

It is so important that we know Him and what is truth. The enemy can portray things that seem so right but be so wrong. What we may think is truth can be a huge deception in our thinking and lives.

Playing with Ouija Boards

Those who are on paranormal TV shows will tell you not to play with the Ouija board, and they are not saying that because they are Christians, but they know this as a fact. It lets in demonic spirits, or what they call negative spirits, in a person or in a place. There is a spiritual realm and when you play in it opens a door that will bring in negative energy or demonic presences, by using this. It is not a simple game people play for fun. The spiritual realm is real! God created the spiritual realm but if we use it wrongly it will give Satan legal rights to use it for his means.

In the Old Testament Saul consulted a woman called the Witch of Endor to summon the spirit of Samuel to receive advice against the Philistines so he could win the battle.

- 1Samuel 28:6 – So Saul inquired of the Lord, but the Lord did not answer him—not by dreams nor by Urim nor by the prophets. 7 So Saul instructed his servants, "Find me a woman who is a medium, so that I may go to her and inquire of her." His servants replied to him, "There is a woman who is a medium in Endor."

The situation did not turn out well for Saul. God tells us not to communicate with the dead in the bible. He tells us this for our own protection. It can open portals (doors) to a dark dimension and a spiritual plane that we know nothing about. We then give these entities a legal right in our home and lives, or even possession, when we open to their realm. I cannot say it enough... playing with a Ouija board is no game!!!!

Other things that are included in being a part of the occult:

Zodiac readings, Ouija board, tarot cards, palm or writing readings, role playing games (like Dungeon and Dragons), séances, crystal balls, crystal pendulum, hypnotism (as it opens our spirit up to anything), Spiritualism, conjuring up spells and magic (regarding magic, I am not talking about illusionists. There is a difference in entertainment and fooling the eye.) Anything that depends on something other than God Himself, can open us up to demons to work in our lives, and in extreme measures on to possession.

If you have ever participated with a Ouija board, called on a medium, shaman, astrology or what is not of God, ask God's forgiveness. This is so no hold or open door can exist from it. The occult realm is nowhere to be playing for fun. It is real and exists. You may think you have power, but in the end, Satan will demand payment for using his realm. It will cost you and your future generations a lot. His blood can redeem these issues in your life, by repenting to God and asking his forgiveness and cutting any hold to the next generations.

Cults/Religions and Other Teachings that are Not of Christ

False teachings and doctrines can impact greatly in our walk with Christ. That is why it is important to know God and His heart. Man since the fall has wanted power, wealth and control over others. They want to be God or like God.

My husband so loved God, but also was so tired of man's religion and his sins in his own life. He was ready to give up on Christianity. One day walking on the beach he bared his heart to God and said he wanted to really know who God is and not man's thinking or ways. If God could not show him, he was done with church and God.

In our western thinking when we ask this, we would expect God to show us just who He is. In Jewish thinking God would show us who He is not. And so, began my husband walk. He ended up going to a bible study led by a woman. She told him things nobody knew about him. He was so astounded by this, he jumped in and was sold, as were others. She set herself up as what she proclaimed to be the

Apostle/Pastor/Prophet. At one point he was instructed that she had prayed, and he was to give 30% of what he made to her and the ministry. There were right things in the ministry, but red flags kept coming up. She recognized he heard God and called him a prophet. One time she told him to prophesy, but he did not want to prophesy something that was not God and was afraid to prophesy falsely. In the old testament when prophets prophesied what was not God they died. Because he did not, she ordered someone to hit him in the stomach hard with a Bible.

She told him and another man that they were lusting after her and both had sexual dreams about her. Both men denied this. Another thing that happened was she told some women that God had told her some of the women were to dance before her in the sanctuary in their under garments, signifying when David danced before the Lord naked. Other things began happening. He fell back into some of his old patterns of sin. He left knowing this was not God and was discouraged. Sometimes people can make something sound so right, but do not believe or be pulled in by deception. Be wise and discerning. If you get a check, go with your first instinct.

- 1 John 4:1 - Beloved, do not believe every spirit, but test the spirits to see whether they are from God, for many false prophets have gone out into the world.
- Deuteronomy 13:1-3 - If a prophet or a dreamer of dreams arises among you and gives you a sign or a

wonder, and the sign or wonder that he tells you comes
to pass, and if he says, 'Let us go after other gods,' which
you have not known, 'and let us serve them,' you shall
not listen to the words of that prophet or that dreamer
of dreams. For the Lord, your God is testing you, to
know whether you love the Lord your God with all your
heart and with all your soul.

Not all prophecy or knowledge is from the gifting of God.
Demons have been around from the beginning of time, first as
angels and then the fall with Lucifer. They are very well organized
and are assigned to people, places, and things. Again, we will know
those who are truly with God by their fruit.

- Galatians 5:22 - But the fruit of the Spirit is love, joy,
  peace, forbearance, kindness, goodness, faithfulness, 23
  gentleness and self-control. Against such things there is
  no law.

Sometimes you will not see who someone truly is or the moti-
vation behind them until later, so be patient and wait till you know
who they are by the fruit of the Spirit. Do not look at all they
seem able to do.

God has given us all a gift of hearing Him. Everyone hears in a
different way, but we all can hear His voice.

- John 10:27 - My sheep listen to my voice; I know them,
  and they follow me.

We just must be aware we can mistake what we are hearing and
think it is God and it ends up being ourselves. It can also be the
enemy speaking to us or bad advice from others. It is not wrong to
search and ask God if something is of Him or not. He has given us
the Holy Spirit and the Bible to balance it all out.

For me hearing God comes in different ways. It is either something that just drops in me and all the sudden I have what I call just a knowing. He uses my heart and a special feeling happen and I just know it is God. He also can speak to us through the bible, prophecy, books, others sharing with us. There are so many ways but balancing it out with the Bible is necessary and asking God for His truth in it.

In the early 80's I was beginning to understand how God would speak to me. There was a couple who always were saying how they were in need. We had 4 children and things were very tight financially. This couple was saying again how in need they were. I decided to go through my cupboards and give ½ of everything we had. When I finished, I noticed a 25-cent piece lying in the center of the floor. It stunned me because I had not noticed it before, and I had just finished vacuuming before I went through my cupboards. A thought hit my mind about going to my bible and reading page 25 in my bible, as it was a 25-cent piece. I thought that is crazy, but to prove it is just me being weird, I went and opened my bible. On page 25 it said...do not go down to Egypt, there is no famine. I thought this is crazy. I still took the food to them. One of my giftings is a mercy person, which can be a negative trait, also. A week later we helped them move and they had a freezer full of food that had been in the freezer for a while as it had frost on it. I learned about lesson paying attention when God speaks. I know he still honored my heart, because it was all done in innocence, but food was not what they needed.

God gives us all a free will. He is not a controlling God. He WILL NOT control us. He gives us our own choices. He loves and wants what is best for each of us. Sometimes it may not be what we want to hear, but He knows what is best for each of His children. Sometimes He allows us to go through His tough love, which is not fun.

God will never go against who He is or control someone to be what He wants. Again, He does not want puppets, but those who truly will love and follow Him. We each have choices to make.

Satan wants to keep us captive and so religiousness comes into play. Whether it comes from another religion, cult, or even those who love Jesus, religion will say we have to try harder, work harder, figure out what we are doing wrong, pray harder, read the bible more, not miss church, be more spiritual, and the list goes on. It is not what we do or not do, but who He is in our life. Jesus gave his life to free and redeem us from the curse of the law. In the Old Testament God laid out Laws for the Jews to follow. He was trying to show them that no one could be perfect and keep all the laws. He had promised a Messiah that would come and be a sacrifice for our sins. They understood sacrifice for sins, because the priests would give animal sacrifices to God to cover the sin of the people. When Jesus came and gave his life as our sacrificial lamb, many missed understanding this. No one can follow and obey 100% of the laws. That is why the sacrificial lamb was sent. Gods' son was given once and for all. This is Gods' act of love and mercy to each of us, the world, and Gods' chosen ones the Jews. But it still is our choice to accept this gift or not. We all come short of the glory of God. When we get to Heaven, we will be surprised of those who we see, or do not see.

We can all be deceived...the bible says even the elect can be deceived. The key is, did we accept Jesus Christ as our personal Savior, who is the gift God himself gave each of us for the reconciliation of what was lost in the Garden during Adam and Eve's time. We also need to understand that many people have been misled and misguided in their understanding of God and what truth is. This does not keep us out of Heaven, but in this life on earth we will be kept in bondage and not walking in total freedom and closeness to God as we could be.

If it were not for the grace of God none of us would be in Heaven. God looks at each individual's heart, and He is the judge, not us. If someone loves Jesus and is misguided, then who are we to say if they get to be in Heaven or not? Every denomination, church, or individual, can be off in their beliefs and some of their doctrinal beliefs. What makes you think you know all truth? No one except God is perfect. Good news is when we come face to face with God, we will have all truth.

We can be in Christian churches or denominations and still have wrong teachings about what is what. But when it comes to other religions: Buddhism, Islam, Hinduism, Shamanism, New Age, Paganism, Spiritualism and all the other religions of the world that do not believe that Jesus is the Messiah, there is a difference. The enemy wants to keep them in blindness and believe they are viewing things rightly. The Bible is clear we are not to worship creation or angels, but God the Creator.

- Romans 1:25- They exchanged the truth about God for a lie and worshiped and served created things rather than the Creator—who is forever praised.

In the 80's in Medford, Oregon a group of Christian people came together and started a study and prayer. As time went on things started happening in the group. They started seeing an angel that would communicate to them. What happened was that 2 of the women ended up murdering some people because this angel told them too. They were following an angel that appeared as an angel of light, but who was demonic. It wanted their worship. Had these two women discerned by what scripture really says about worshiping anything other than God, they would have known this was not God. They worshiped this angel as if it were God and were deceived.

- Rev. 22: 8, 9 - I, John, am the one who heard and saw these things. And when I had heard and seen them, I fell-down to worship at the feet of the angel who had been showing them to me. 9 But he said to me, "Don't do that! I am a fellow servant with you and with your fellow prophets and with all who keep the words of this scroll. Worship God!

- Colossians 2:18 - See to it that no one takes you captive
  through hollow and deceptive philosophy, which
  depends on human tradition and the elemental spiritual
  forces of this world rather than on Christ.

The enemy twists the truth and other religions come into being. Only God knows the outcome of each of our souls in the end. We still are to love as Christ loves. He died for all mankind.

I love what Mother Teresa said. She said that Christ gave his life for all mankind and she chooses to serve Christ in each one of them, whether they know Him or not. Even during her life, with all she did for others, she still felt she had not done enough for God. It is not what we do, or what we do not do, but it is who He is.

Most of the major religions in the world will say they believe Jesus was a prophet of God. Their sacred books talk about Jesus being a prophet. If they believe this, then a

Prophet of God would not lie. How can they explain the passage of scripture in John 14:6 that states: "I am the Way, the Truth, and the Life. No one comes to the Father except through Me." This is Jesus' words. A prophet will not lie, so the conclusion is if they call him a prophet, then what He said must be truth. Know this, we never know who in the last moment of their breath on earth, received Jesus.

Ghost Hunting

Although ghost hunting is interesting & alluring to many, I would stay out of this arena. It has become an extremely popular thing and there are many TV shows about this. Biblically, God says not to dabble in this.

- Saul called on the witch of Endor to contact Samuel
  who was dead. Saul disobeyed God and his life was
  taken because of his disobedience for calling a witch in

and calling up the dead. God was not happy – Samuel 28: 3-25.

- Deuteronomy 18:10 – There shall not be found among you anyone who burns his son or his daughter as an offering, anyone who practices divination or tells fortunes or interprets omens, or a sorcerer 11 or a charmer or a medium or a necromancer *or one who inquires of the dead.*

In the early 90's, our family decided to go on a vacation together. We decided to tour the Oregon coast. I love history and the Victorian era, so we decided to take a tour of the founder's home in one of the coastal cities. When we pulled up to the house, my daughter said, "That place is haunted." I rolled my eyes and felt she did not know what she was talking about. I said, "Please don't ruin what I would like to see."

When we entered the house, immediately I knew that the deceased children in the home had been molested. I remember thinking, "Why did that feeling come on so strong to me?" Then the tour guide said there were 2 girl children who never married. I felt that I knew why. I also felt he was abusive. The guide then talked about how the father was known as a very harsh and strong personality. The guide talked about how séances were held in the home during the owner's time there. I thought, "Great, ugh!" When we went upstairs to the bedroom of the father, I became very nauseated and could not breathe normally. I told my husband I needed to leave. We left.

Later that day we stopped at another pastor's house, who we knew and lived in the area. We shared we had taken a tour of this home. I did not tell them of the experience. They asked, "Did you know that house was haunted?"

For three days I was miserable. My mind and my inner spirit were being pulled back to that house. What was there was trying to pull me in with an obsession about the occupants of the home. I kept praying the blood of Jesus over my mind and spirit. After the third day I finally was free from whatever was pulling me back there. I learned that even on vacation, I cannot let my spiritual senses down, and learned that supernatural entities can pull on anyone. I will never again enter a place that I know is haunted, because of how sensitive I am to the spiritual realm.

Years later I was in a bookstore where I currently live and picked up a book to look at it. It was a book on the founder of that coastal city I just shared about. In the book it talked about how he was related to Clark (of the Lewis & Clark Expedition), and how Clark would visit this man. Funny thing is, on my 2 X Great Grandmother's side, I am related to Clark of Lewis and Clark. Is this why there was such a connection when I entered the home? I do not know, but that would be remarkably interesting to know if being related, I picked up on things easier.

We know there is life beyond where we are now. The Bible tells us things about Heaven, but we do not know a lot about what exists in the next phase of the after- life. There are scriptures in the Old Testament concerning Abraham's bosom, where those that have passed were in waiting. When Jesus was on the cross, he told the thief next to Him he would join Him in Paradise. Then there are scriptures on Heaven itself. It would be interesting to do a biblical study on this, but until we pass to the other side we will probably never know or understand how everything works.

With all that the paranormal people are getting into, the question is, are ghost just spirits/energy of people who have passed and have not moved on. Or are the ghosts really demons manifesting themselves as ghost. I believe they can be one or the other. Paranormal investigators will tell you not to ghost hunt, unless you know what you are doing. There are a lot of stories from the ghost hunters where these spirits and demonic spirits have attached to the people hunting for ghost and have followed them home. It raised havoc in their lives and within their families.

In 2010 my husband and I moved to Idaho to retire. We purchased a wonderful 2 story home with 5 bedrooms. We had been in the home for about a month, and one late night when we were asleep the smoke alarm sounded off in our bedroom. My husband went and got a ladder, because of the high ceilings. Nothing seemed strange, this does happen with smoke detectors. There was no fire, but maybe a spider had gotten into the mechanism. We had just changed the battery to all the smoke alarms in the house, so we thought it could be a bad battery or connection. This alarm was one that was wired into the home and had a back - up battery, which we had replaced. My husband pulled the battery out, and the detector continues making the shrill alert sound. He then unattached the whole smoke alarm from the electrical plug in the ceiling. It had no power or battery and for an unreasonable amount of time, it continued making the noise. It dawned on me this is not normal. I immediately spoke the blood of Jesus over the whole situation. The fire alarm stops immediately and all the sudden the intercom that we have in the home came on and we heard a man and a woman's voice having a serious conversation. To this day I do not know what that was. We prayed throughout the home, anointed with oil, and prayed over the property and boundary lines. We have not had anything like that happen since. Fear is one thing that increases the power in the supernatural realm. If things happen beyond what you anticipate, stay out of fear. Fear is not from the God. Yes, there is a healthy fear of things and of God Himself, but the feeling of nothing to help is a lie, God is always there and knows what you are facing. Faith is believing God can do all things if He chooses. He knows and loves us.

In the spiritual realm, things happen. People have been so sheltered, but with TV, U tube, books and other media a lot that was not known is now becoming known. We have phones with instance picture taking and video taking. Things cannot stay hidden as they could in the past. People are catching things that were not seen by the eyes but appear in pictures and videos. Yes, some are hoaxes, but some cannot be disproven.

Just recently I watched a video on Animal Planet. It also was on U tube. A guy was riding his 3-wheeler in the middle of a shallow river. He is having a blast and the next thing you see, a head of him is a mist forming and a Big Foot Creature walking across the river into the mist but does not come out the other side of the mist. The mist disappears and nothing there. This opens a lot of questions... Was it somehow staged or was this real?

Scientists are saying now they can prove there is another dimension next to ours. Is this so? Is this what is being called a portal for demons and the dead? In these times it is so important we keep our eyes on Jesus. Nothing is as it was before. We are living in a distorted time. More and more, strange things are being recorded and photographed because of the technology we now have. It is hard to know what is real and what is not. People are carrying their phones and have ready access to take videos and pictures with it. Before we would only hear of people experiences and these would become passed from mouth or legends began from the experiences.

Sometimes just once praying can take care of things that are spiritually off. Other times more may need to happen to break an area of strongholds. It is important to deal in these areas with someone who understands God is the only way. Again, any other power, than the power of God can give the enemy a right to many things.

- Exodus 20:3 and Deuteronomy 5:7 say – You shall have no other gods before me.

For me, it is best just to stay out of these realms, unless something manifests, and you need help. With paranormal problems people will call in ghost hunters, mediums, psychics, shamans, wiccin, and other occult people. It may seem like the problems are taken care of, but worse things can come. The dark side of spiritual things always cost you in the long run and you have given permission darkness to have more power. It is important to seek someone who loves God, knows how to deal in this realm, and uses only things of God to deal with it. We must remember using other ways may have an affect right off, and seem to take care of the situation, but the enemy *will* demand payback. It is a deception.

What we Bring in Our Homes

Antiques can be things spirits can attach themselves to. Or things we may bring in our home from other countries. Any time we bring something into our home that I am not sure about or comfortable, I pray over it and break off anything that is attached. This is wisdom. There are many stories about people bringing things home from estate sales, 2nd hand places, other countries, or even family heirlooms and supernatural things in their homes begin to manifest.

What we allow in our homes by music, TV, even certain people can bring a wrong atmosphere into our homes. Our homes need to be our sanctuary and safe place. We need to repent to the Lord and pray through our homes on a regular basis, anointing with oil and covering our homes, family, and lives in the blood of Christ. What we do not realize is the world knows this and uses other things like sage and prayers to their gods. Christians need to understand how to keep their homes clean spiritually and be wise what they let in.

My mother had Alzheimer's and lived with us for 17 years. She was a dear sweet lady. We needed to leave a short time to do business in another state. We had a dear friend who was recognized all over the World as a Prophet. He mentored many well- known Prophets. I had a friend who was coming in to stay with my mom. She ended up not able to stay with her, so someone else I knew came in to stay. The Prophet told us not to let that woman in our home, about 6 months prior. I was not understanding why he has said that to us. Forgetting about it, this woman came and stayed to help my mom. It turned out in chaos. My mom calling daily to me and my young granddaughter, who was staying with us, calling me. I learned even though we may not understand at the time, we need to take seriously when the Lord speaks. A lesson well learned.

A friend out of her heart opened their home up to someone needing a place to stay. The woman had feelings for the husband in the past. The husband was unaware of this, but the wife picked up on it. The woman still had feelings for the husband. The enemy wants to destroy marriages and people. Things were dealt with and the woman had to leave. A spiritual tie with someone can leave a door open, even if in the past. We so need to watch the spiritual things we allow in our homes.

Do Aliens Exist?

There are two thoughts on this:

Science says there is, and many think Area-51 is holding back information on this. There are those who claim to be abducted by aliens. There are those who believe they are already living among us. Remember though that fallen angels can make things seem true and give an experience, that seems real for a person. They can make things look as though they are not. So, I am still asking God what the truth is.

There does seem to be more and more sightings and photo evidence that they exist. Especially with our devices being so ready in our hands to take pictures and video's.

So, is there other life in other places? Or are the demonic entities making it look like alien beings do exist? Did demons appear to ancient cultures so they would worship something other than God? Or did God create other life on other planets? Only God knows. The answers to this area of things are not solid. Many believe these are demons, and many believe there is life on other planets in other galaxies. I bring this up, so again, you can understand that the enemy will and can use all things to look like truth. Until we are 100% sure, it could be either way. We need to trust God with all that is unknown to us. No matter what the answer is, He is in control of it all! We do not need to be in fear of the unknown, for He is the Creator. Our trust is totally in Him on anything unknown. We have no fear because of who our God is.

Use of Drugs and Alcohol

When people abuse drugs or alcohol, using them to dull feelings, or just to get high, can open a door for the demonic to have a hold in their life.

The Greek word for drug is "Pharmakeia", which when translated means "demonic". This is where we get our English word pharmaceutical (Pharmacy). This does not mean medicine is wrong. But we need to be aware how things affect our body and use wisely. Rather they man-made or natural, medicine or drugs are medicine. Natural medications can hurt the body just as the man-made ones. A patient went in for a minor surgery. He forgot to tell the doctor about a natural medicine he was taking. It interacted with the anesthesia and he died. It was a natural medication. All can interact with other medications or things. Pharmacists go to school much longer than most doctors. So, it is wise to check with what you are taking, both natural and man-made. I was Triage for 8 doctors for 5 years and was amazed how unknowledgeable the public can be in this area.

If you look up scriptures on drinking wine, they will tell us a little is fine.

- 1Timothy 5:23 – (No longer drink only water but use a little wine for the sake of your stomach and your frequent ailments.)
- Ecclesiastes 9:7 – Go, eat your bread with joy, and drink your wine with a merry heart, for God has already approved what you do.

But scriptures warn us about getting drunk:

- 1Peter 4:3 – For the time that is past suffices for doing what the Gentiles want to do, living in sensuality, passions, *drunkenness*, orgies, *drinking parties*, and lawless idolatry.

- Ephesians 5:18 – And do not get drunk with wine, for that is debauchery, but be filled with the Spirit...

God is a protective parent. He wants us safe, so He warns us about drunkenness and putting our bodies in that state where we can potentially open the door to negative spiritual things and health issues.

When we abuse these substances, our inhibitions disappear. It is extremely easy then for demonic spirits to gain control and enter through this door. We then become vulnerable to demonic strongholds that can take over our lives and destroy us and those around us. This is what happens in addiction. Saying we cannot get addicted is the first lie that the enemy of our soul wants us to believe.

Science already agrees that substances easily can take over our lives and rule our emotions and minds. The feeling that we may have while we are high is not a reality. It does not take care of our hurts or longings. Only God can come in heal and fill our empty areas.

I have four children. Three are biological and one by adoption. She came to us 4 years old and already had lived a lifetime of baggage. She is now 38 and finally has begun her healing of trying to mask all her hurts and feelings with alcohol and drugs. Early years are so important for children. The other three children never went into to alcohol and drugs. I am so proud of her, as addictions are so hard to overcome. But it can be done when the person decides to end the cycle. She said she finally let God become her center. Her journey has been hard but so rewarding.

Control

Fleshly control is a form of witchcraft. God does not control us, and neither should we control others, let others control us or situations, or make our agenda in situations that involve others. God hates control.

Here He is God, and He gives us each our own choices and ways. There were laws placed in order at the time of creation, and these come into play if we do not choose rightly, but God still gives us free choice.

Controllers can be either men or women. They like position and power over others. They can be ministers, our spouses, or just in the world where we walk or work in. There are three ways that control expresses itself: manipulation, intimidation and domination. Usually, the person with the control issue is so insecure, has deep fear, and the only way they feel secure is being in power over people and things.

A humble person does not abuse his authority or position, but sees himself as a servant, and is open to discussion, correction, and willing to make sacrifices for others. They trust God over all.

- Philippians 2:3-4 – Do nothing from selfish ambition or conceit, but in humility count others more significant than yourselves.

A marriage is a partnership and should be treated as that. It should be a working together in all situations. No one should be lording anything over another. The church has taught such a wrong view of the marriage. God took a rib from Adam's side and created Eve. A woman should be one with man, at his side. Not under his feet.

If my husband and I do not come to an agreement, then I will respect my husband and trust God through him if it is not a controlling situation. He still is my covering. Does not mean I am less but shows the order of what God laid out. In return he respects me and knows God created me to be his balance, and him mine.

Control is a form of witchcraft. It tries to gain what it wants by with-holding from another (i.e., money, sex), uses manipulation, or abuse physically or emotionally to control a situation or person. When a person is controlled that person will become a shell of a person because of the witchcraft being used against them.

I have a very dear friend. She had been through a lot through her life. Because of many surgeries she became addicted to prescription drugs. The husband was tight with money given to the household expenses. Both had things that opened them and their marriage up into wrong things, her addictions and his pornography and control issues. If you met them, you would like them both. As time went on his control issues got worse because of his fear of her spending money. We had not seen each other for a few years. When I saw her, she was a shell of a person. I am happy to say she is now free from addiction and happy. Her addiction and his control did this to her. Her husband still has a hard time understanding he was at fault too. Unfortunately, the marriage ended. We, without understanding, can open our homes up to wrong things with what we allow in, his control and pornography, and her addictions.

Sex: Other than What God Approves

Pornography, sexual activities outside of marriage, homosexuality, lusting, masturbation (having sex with yourself), incest, and rape open doors for the enemy and give demonic holds a right to hold us captive. It is so important to wait to give oneself sexually on the marriage night.

I married at 17. I did not keep myself sexually pure. It really opened doors in the marriage. And of course, he was not faithful through the years. When I married, I was committed for life and it was so heartbreaking that did not happen. God restored me and brought a wonderful gift of a husband into my life. We waited till married till we were intimate. What a difference in the marriage. We have an innocence that was never there in my first marriage. We both became virgins again, spiritually. I so love our marriage and it is healthy and beautiful.

God created sex as a spiritual bond to seal and tie together two people in a marriage. It is about when "two become one". It produces a soul tie to our mate for life.

When we go beyond that protection God laid in place is, we open doors. When we give ourselves to others outside of marriage, we miss- use that special gift given specifically by God to unite a marriage. When we have sex with someone, we then become soul tied to who we have given our self to sexually. We end up in a spiritual tie to someone. Not only are we tied to that person, but also those they have had sex with outside of marriage. It becomes a domino effect to all those they have had sex with and made a soul tie with. We then wonder why we feel so splintered and not our self. God created this intimacy special for marriage so the two can become one. Not splintered to everyone else. Soul ties are extraordinarily strong because God created it. With holding your virginity till marriage, it creates a bond, innocence, and purity to the marriage. If you have crossed this boundary, ask God's forgiveness. And sin no more. Have someone you trust pray and break off any soul ties you have created unknowingly. Keep yourself pure and you will become a whole person again instead of a person split in so many ways.

- John 8: 4-11 – they said to Jesus, "Teacher, this woman has been caught in the act of adultery. 5 Now in the Law, Moses commanded us to stone such women. So, what do you say?" 6 This they said to test him, that they might have some charge to bring against him. Jesus bent down and wrote with his finger on the ground. 7 And as they continued to ask him, he stood up and said to them, "Let him who is without sin among you be the first to throw a stone at her." 8 And once more he bent down and wrote on the ground. 9 But when they heard it, they went away one by one, beginning with the older ones, and Jesus was left alone with the woman standing before him. 10 Jesus stood up and said to her, "Woman, where are they? Has no one condemned you?" 11 She said, "No one, Lord." And Jesus said, "Neither do I condemn you; go, and from now on sin no more.

Pornography

Once you start looking at porn, doors are opened, it pulls you in, slow at first, and addiction begins. Once that happens, it leads you down the road even deeper. It starts with fantasy and eventually pulls the person into deeper sexual sin. It is perversion and lust.

When watching a Dr. Phil show on pornography, Dr. Phil said it so well. He asked a man who was involved with pornography, "How he would feel if other men were looking at your daughter in a nude photo, which had been posed for." The man said, "No way." Dr. Phil then said in a strong way, "Then why are you looking at someone else's daughter?" "That is somebody's daughter."

Pornography is having an affair with someone other than your spouse. It gives way to fantasy and wrong imaginations and opens the door for the enemy to enter your life and addiction begins. It begins, but then lusts for more. What was just porn turns into sexual addictions that destroy lives. It is so important to protect your eyes from what they see –

- Matthew 6:22-23 - The eye is the lamp of the body. If your eyes are healthy, your whole body will be full of light. 23 But if your eyes are unhealthy, your whole body will be full of darkness. If then the light within you is darkness, how great is that darkness!

The enemy is not stupid. He has allowed the movie industry, what we see on television, online availability, to lure men and women into this fantasy. People need to be set free from this. You will eventually get exposed. Just how this sin works. God will not allow unfaithfulness of any kind with Him or your spouse.

Adultery & Fornication

Sex outside of marriage – Exodus 20:14; Hebrews 13:4, 1Thessalonians 4:3; Colossians 3: 5&6.

God created intimacy between a husband and wife. Not outside marriage. God loves us enough to protect us. Being intimate with your marriage convent partner was set up by God as a special intimate tie to our mate. Our souls become one. God created it this way to keep a purity and innocence in the marriage.

When infidelity happens, the purity and innocence is gone, and the marriage usually never can get back to the innocence that once was there. It produces serious cracks and mistrust issues and will never have the purity again. It takes a lot for marriages to work through this kind of betrayal.

Therefore, the enemy puts emotional attractions between others so he can destroy people, marriages, families, and the children involved. Only God can resurrect the pain and damage from this. It is so important to keep your marriage bed undefiled.

The enemy will use anything to bring hurt and distrust in a marriage. Even an emotional tie that is not physical.

A husband and wife were going through a hard area in their marriage. They loved each other but trying to put a blended household together. Both had children. To help a friend they decided to let her move in with her son for a while.

Everything was fine for a while, but the woman had been friends with the husband before they married. The other woman and husband started talking about the problems in the marriage. Before long there was an emotional attachment.

I feel more by the female than the male, but it still put a lot of tensions between husband and wife. Wife could see it, husband could not. The woman moved out.

No sexual ties had happened, so they were able to move on quickly. I believe the husband had no clue. But the woman knew exactly what she was doing.

Pray protection and seal the blood of Jesus around your

marriage and your mate. If infidelity happens, get help. Do not think it will just be fixed. Counseling and communication are key in this area.

Before marriage repent for those you have made soul ties to in the past and ask God's forgiveness ask that your marriage bed be pure and not bring any past relationships into it.

What a lot of people do not understand is that when we become intimate with someone, we open our being, our soul, and demonic spirits can transfer from one person to another. Whenever we have sexual contact with someone, we make soul ties with that person.

This is how a door opens and we give permission for something not of God to come in.

Every person you have ever slept with, you now have a spiritual soul tie connection with. You wonder why you never are feeling whole with in your-self.

That is why prayer is needed to break the soul ties of others that are not your mate and any demonic spirit that may have transferred and attached to you from others.

Flirting is cheating. It breaks a boundary within a committed relationship.

In a committed relationship we agree to give certain parts of ourselves to our partner. When we flirt, we are attracted to that individual and we are giving sexual interest and attention that only our partner should have.

I am also careful about who I lay hands on and who lays hands on me, because of transference of a wrong spirit. Always ask God and go with your gut feelings.

- 1 Timothy 5:22 Be in no hurry to lay hands on people to dedicate them to the Lord's service. Take no part in the sins of others; keep yourself pure.

A husband and wife knew a lady from their church and started being friends.

One day the woman came over to use their washer and dryer. The wife was gone. The husband and this woman started talking. The man said that all the sudden he felt something hit him inside in the stomach.

They started having feelings for each other. And you guessed the rest.

I feel what happened was a transference of a spirit. If we could only see in the spiritual realm and realize what things really are, we would not go that way.

Incest

Sex with those related (even by marriage).

Please note: God does not condemn the person who is a victim of someone raping them or taking advantage, in this way. The sinner is the one who is the perpetrator. The victim is not responsible if underage or were not agreeing to the situation.

This sin seems to be passed down generational lines and has holds on families or they have been a victim in the past. If the perpetrator was a victim in their past, I wonder if a spirit was transferred.

I do not have all the answers but know Inner healing is essential for this and maybe prayer beyond deliverance.

- Leviticus 18:6-8 'No one is to approach any close relative to have sexual relations. I am the Lord. 7 "'Do not dishonor your father by having sexual relations with your mother. She is your mother; do not have relations with her. 8 "'Do not have sexual relations with your father's wife; that would dishonor your father.
- Deuteronomy 27: 22, 23 Cursed is anyone who sleeps with his sister, the daughter of his father or the daughter of his mother. 23 Cursed is anyone who sleeps with his mother-in-law.

Rape

In these cases, it is the rapist who answers to God. Not the innocent victim. It is important, however, to pray for the victim for healing and breaking any soul ties that could have happened. Both rape and incest are a violation to a person. Not only prayer is needed, but professional help that can help them walk them through this.

Homosexuality

Sex with the same gender.

- Romans 1:26 – 28 – Because of this, God gave them over to shameful lusts. Even their women exchanged natural sexual relations for unnatural ones. 27 In the same way the men also abandoned natural relations with women and were inflamed with lust for one another. Men committed shameful acts with other men and received in themselves the due penalty for their error.
- I Timothy 1:8-11- We know that the law is good if one uses it properly. 9 We also know that the law is made not for the righteous but for lawbreakers and rebels, the ungodly and sinful, the unholy and irreligious, for those who kill their fathers or mothers, for murderers, 10 for the sexually immoral, for those practicing homosexuality, for slave traders and liars and perjurers— and for whatever else is contrary to the sound doctrine 11 that conforms to the gospel concerning the glory of the blessed God, which he entrusted to me.
- I Corinthians 6: 9-11 – Or do you not know that wrongdoers will not inherit the kingdom of God? Do not be deceived: Neither the sexually immoral nor idolaters nor adulterers nor men who have sex with men[a] 10 nor thieves nor the greedy nor drunkards nor

slanderers nor swindlers will inherit the kingdom of God. 11 And that is what some of you were. But you were washed, you were sanctified, you were justified in the name of the Lord Jesus Christ and by the Spirit of our God.

- Leviticus 20:13 – If a man has sexual relations with a man as one does with a woman, both have done what is detestable.

The one thing we need to remember is that Homosexuality, Adultery, Lust, is all put together in the same scripture as a Liar and Thief. I believe that is to show us that in God's eyes all sin is the same. Each sin has a different way it plays out in God's law, but to Him we are all sinners. We must never believe we are better than those who sin. We too, are sinners in God's eyes. We must love the sinner, but not the sin, and let God be the judge. We need wisdom and direction how to minister to each person God brings in our lives. Usually, homosexuality is from deep hurts and wounds. They are now saying scientifically how we are made. I do not know if I agree with this. All I know is God's word says it is wrong.

In the mid 80's, we were pastoring a church in East Texas. A lot of the leadership could not grasp that a Christian could have demonic holds in them. They only believed Christians could be oppressed but not have a demonic hold.

We had a young woman come who was in her 30's. Single, loved the Lord with all her heart and was the most zealous one in the church. She loved people. And loved God.

One night she asked me to meet her down at the building where the church was located. She cleaned the church once every week for us and called me to please meet her there. She was going through some hard things and needed to talk.

There was a hallway that led to the sanctuary side of the building. I came around the corner and she grabbed me, turned me around and held me straight up against the wall, one handed, with my feet dangling. I was 2 x's her weight. I could see the hate in her eyes. Her eyes were black and glossy, no white in them. Her teeth were clenched, and she was seething. I immediately realized this was not her. It was demonic. All I could do was keep telling her I loved her in the name of Jesus and calling her by her name. Then I remembered about using the blood of Jesus. I started speaking that over her and suddenly, she dropped me and fell to the ground. The Holy Spirit literally plastered her to the ground, and she could not move. I kept speaking the blood of Jesus over her. She kept screaming and squealing in a deep voice that was not her. I was concerned about someone coming into the building that was not associated with the church. The church had half the building. The other half was commercial businesses. I decided to drag her by her feet into the sanctuary. The demon in her kept screaming, "No, no, it burns, it burns. I do not want to go in there." It screamed a hideous scream about how it was burning in the fire. Later I realized that the demon did not want to be in God's presence that resided in the sanctuary.

I continued praying over her in the sanctuary. The demon in her growled, spit on me, and cursed me. She was plastered to the floor by the Holy Spirit and could not get up. By God's providence, one of the elders from the church showed up and called the other elders in. We saw deliverance happen for her, but it was just the beginning of God setting her free. The elders became believer's that night in what we were trying to teach them about the demonic and Christians. All I can say is God can use anything to make believers out of not believing in something.

It turned out she was trying to come out of lesbianism. In my understanding, she had not been in a relationship for a long time. We knew she needed help beyond what we could do and called another pastor in, for her. She ended up on the front of Charisma magazine with a well- known pastor ministering to her. All you could see were her tennis shoes and legs, with the pastor kneeling facing her.

It can be extremely hard to set someone free from a perverted spirit. It takes love and patience. This type of demonic hold can be

THE DOORS WE OPEN

transferred by sexual abuse, incest, or perversion coming down a generational line (See generational curses).

In the scientific world they are trying to prove it is a genetic disorder and mess up. In scripture it says, God is against having sex with the same sex, but nothing is ever mentioned about genetic disorders being a sin. So, until God says different, I believe it is not in His will. Again though, we need to understand sin is sin and we are not above anyone.

- John 9:2-3 – His disciples asked him, "Rabbi, who
  sinned, this man or his parents, that he was born blind?"
  3 "Neither this man nor his parents sinned," said Jesus,
  ... but again, it does say that laying down with the same
  sex as a man and a woman do, is sin.

Masturbation

Ephesians 5:3.

The bible does not use the specific word masturbation. Masturbation is having sex with oneself.

I had a friend who loved God and because of health issues there had been no intimacy in the marriage for years. She decided to give herself permission for doing this because of lack of intimacy in her marriage and had some Christians saying it was not sin in her situation.

A few months later her spouse passed. What happened is she opened a door she did not know how to shut. It awakened in her something that God had allowed to be dormant.

She started having desires as she continued with this and ended up in a situation she would have never dreamed of. It opened a door that she could not control in herself.

We think how can this be harmful, but when we open doors that should not be opened, we can bring stuff in that we would never conceive of happening.

Unforgiveness, Anger, and Jealousy Toward Others

Not forgiving, holding on to an offense, bitterness, hatred, jealousy, and anger can open a door to the demonic in your life –

- Galatians 5:21 – The acts of the flesh are obvious: sexual immorality, impurity and debauchery; 20 idolatry and witchcraft; hatred, discord, jealousy, fits of rage, selfish ambition, dissensions, factions 21 and envy; drunkenness, orgies, and the like. I warn you, as I did before, that those who live like this will not inherit the kingdom of God.

Keeping unforgiveness within us and thinking we have the right to carry animosities against another will put us in bondage and will keep us chained in bondage to the person we are holding things against.

With this we have let that person have control over us. That person usually is totally unaware of holding us captive. It is our doing, not theirs.

- Matthew 6:14-15 – For if you forgive other people when they sin against you, your heavenly Father will also forgive you. 15 But if you do not forgive others their sins, your Father will not forgive your sins.
- Ephesians 4:31-32 – Get rid of all bitterness, rage and anger, brawling and slander, along with every form of malice. 32 Be kind and compassionate to one another, forgiving each other, just as in Christ God forgave you.
- Mark 11:25 – And when you stand praying, if you hold anything against anyone, forgive them, so that your Father in heaven may forgive you your sins.
- Colossians 3:8 – But now you must also rid yourselves of all such things as these: anger, rage, malice, slander, and filthy language from your lips.

- Galatians 5:22-23 – But the fruit of the Spirit is love, joy, peace, forbearance, kindness, goodness, faithfulness, gentleness and self-control. Against such things there is no law.

Our flesh is ugly, and it can open doors to cause havoc and stop the blessings of God in our lives. It is so important to forgive others. This does not mean we forget, or bring them back into our lives, but we can forgive and set ourselves free and stop walking in the ways of the flesh.

Forgiving others does not mean they deserve forgiveness but forgive because **YOU** deserve peace in your life.

Most people have not had the best childhoods. Some people's childhood was a lot worse than others.

My husband grew up in an alcoholic family. His mom and dad divorced when he was 9 years old. He and his sister would have to take their wagon down to the tavern and go in to get money for groceries, because of no food was in the home.

It got to the point that his sister and him lived in a home by themselves, down the street from his mother's new husband and his kids. The house had no electricity, and they were 10 and 12. They would go up to where their mother was living to eat dinner.

In today's society their mother would have been placed in prison for neglect.

My husband was angry through a lot of his life regarding his childhood, until he began to understand, that his mother did the best she could with her hurts and unhealed areas from her childhood. He forgave her and felt so free in his life and they ended up having a wonderful relationship in her last years.

Parents end up parenting through unhealed areas in their lives. We may or may not know what they walked through.

It is so important we become healed, so the next generation does not have the same issues to pass down to their children. Most realize this too late, but forgiveness and restoration are the key.

You may not have had perfect parents. Perfect parents do not exist. They were once children of imperfect parents. There is no excuse for abuse, but there is room for growth. It is generational, situational, environmental, accidental, in a time period, and it can be intentional. As adults we must let it go.

They most likely have been punished enough of their memories of what happened. Seek what was good and accept you did not have perfect parents. Accept their failings and forgive them.

By doing this you can find freedom in your life ahead.

Relationships

The enemy loves to pull us into things that causes temptation or with people that could cause us to open doors. The enemy then gains access to our lives. What people are seeking is because of a void inside them.

- 1Corinthians 15:33 - Do not be misled: Bad company corrupts good character.

Wrong relationships can pull us into wrong things and take us further away from God. We need to surround ourselves with those who have the same mind in Christ.

- 2 Corinthians 6:13-15 - Do not be yoked together with unbelievers. For what do righteousness and wickedness have in common? Or what fellowship can light have with darkness? 15 What harmony is there between Christ and Belial? Or what does a believer have in common with an unbeliever?

This does not mean we are to isolate ourselves to be only with believers. Christ tells us to bring His love to the world. Those who are new in Christ or those who have pasts, and certain weakness, need to use wisdom and be careful. If a past alcoholic, someone else may be called to enter places to bring people to

Christ. Do not be prideful and think you have it, and nothing can happen.

People seem to think happiness is having a mate or friendship. Happiness starts with you. Not with a relationship, your job, or friends. Christ is the only one who can fill that void. He created a void in us where only He can fulfill. No person, place or thing will ever fill it.

We need to evaluate who, what, and where we spend time. We can either have healthy things surround us or negative things that can pull us into wrong choices and thinking.

One thing I learned walking with God, that to be closer in relationship with Him I had to leave performance behind. Religion says we must be this way or that way. He already gave His life for us. All He asks is for us to open our heart to Him. It is nothing about how we perform or not perform. He wants a relationship with us.

Inner Vows We Make

Inner vows are another way we open doors. These are sober minded things we make deep within ourselves. Stating that we will not become like someone or not do things we have watched someone do. Like I will never be like my father or mother.

Or I will never make that mistake or be like them.

What happens is we come into an agreement with judgment. When we make these inner vows, we can become exactly what we did not want to be. This can start a chain reaction in us. We find ourselves not able to maintain close relationships, not able to trust, not able to give our whole heart to someone, or becoming exactly like our parents, which we did not want. Or things happening in our lives we never thought possible.

I will not extend a lot about this, because excellent books are on this subject. Inner healing, and understanding God are available by John L. Sandford through Elijah House Ministry online or from a bookstore. I highly recommend his books. Understanding about inner healing can set us free from things that keep us from becoming who we were created to be.

The interesting thing is that many things the Lord gave John and Paula Sanford, regarding inner healing, are being used in Psychiatry today. God gave them valuable gems to help heal others. There is no way I can do justice to what teachings God brought to them. Please invest and read these. John and Paula were so balanced and real with learning and writing what God taught them. Healing for soul, mind and body. This is so needed into days society. Go online to elijahhouse.org.

Generational Sins and Curses

Generation sins or curse, coming down through our blood line, can be the root cause of many things in our lives. Your ancestors and the future generations can be held captive by other people sins in the family line. We can open doors that play out in our children's lives, our grandchildren's lives, up to 4 generations. We also can cause good things to happen to the generations after us, by following Jesus and living the life He has called us to. By breaking off generational sins and curses that have come down the blood line and calling back in the good things of God in that person's blood line can bring an end to a tie of sin and make the future generations free from a past generations sin.

My husband was given a dream by the Lord. In the dream he was walking with God in a meadow and God told him He was going to take him down in a cave. In this cave were jail cells with open doors. In two of the cells, he knew that one was his dad, and the other was his grandfather. They did not understand that they could walk out. The Lord started talking to him about the generational sins that hold a person captive. Through all this my husband understood that we ourselves keep ourselves in captivity. The doors are open for us to walk through and not take up the sins of our forefathers. So powerful! Through Christ we are set free, because of His sacrifice on the cross.

Exodus 34:7 states that iniquity from a father can come down on the children and their children to the third and fourth generation.

It can bring physical sickness, emotional sickness, or spiritual sickness that will keep us from moving forward in our lives. Many things can be passed down through the lineage and blood lines.

All the wrong things can be broken off with praying the blood of Jesus over the person's life, asking forgiveness for our ancestor's sins and putting them to death at the cross of Jesus.

We all are affected by things that have been passed down from our ancestors, both good and bad. You have a God-given inheritance that belongs to you and it is the time to call them back into your blood line.

- Exodus 20:5 – You shall not bow down to them or worship them; for I, the Lord your God, am a jealous God, punishing the children for the sin of the parents to the third and fourth generation of those who hate me...
- Exodus 34:7 maintaining love to thousands, and forgiving wickedness, rebellion and sin. Yet he does not leave the guilty unpunished; he punishes the children and their children for the sin of the parents to the third and fourth generation.
- Numbers 14:18 – 18 'The Lord is slow to anger, abounding in love and forgiving sin and rebellion. Yet he does not leave the guilty unpunished; he punishes the children for the sin of the parents to the third and fourth generation.

Using prayer to ask God to break the generational sins and bring in the good things and gifts God created down through your blood line, can set you free, and the next generation.

- Romans 8:1-2 – Therefore, there is now no condemnation for those who are in Christ Jesus, 2 because through Christ Jesus the law of the Spirit who gives life has set you free from the law of sin and death.

Lies and Deception

Satan and his demons lie. They whisper in our minds about what someone may be thinking, or how someone is doing something behind our backs. How they are gossiping about us, and so on. The demons want to take away our confidence so we cannot become or do our best. For me, the easiest thing to do is to face our beliefs. I may go to someone and ask them if everything is all right between us. If they say yes, then I was being lied to. If not and they still say yes, then it is between them and God. Making peace is so important.

Satan loves to lie to us about ourselves. I remember in my late 20's while I was standing in the bathroom doing my hair, God spoke to my heart and said, "Do you love yourself?" At that time in my life, I was so insecure about myself, so I said, "No God I do not!" Gently He said to me, "How can you not love my creation?" That day I had a new revelation. My heart can be ugly sometimes, but it is not about what I think is beauty, it is what He thinks, because I am His creation. I answered back and said, "Yes Lord, I love the creation you created."

The biggest battleground we face is the battle in our minds. This is Satan's easiest way for him to have access to us. That is why it is so important to know who God is, know God's heart, and what scripture tells us. We not only need to get it in our minds, but down solid in our hearts, so we become unshakeable.

If we start believing the lies that come in our mind and think others are doing or saying things without proof of truth, we become in bondage to the lie and bind ourselves to others emotionally. One minister/prophet once said to me, "Some will, some won't, so what! What a profound statement. It has helped me walk through a lot with people, understanding that it is not my problem to carry or worry about what others may think.

When people lie and deceive it does not only affect the one doing it but affects those around these people. The one lying must keep up with who they have told what to. They then must lie to cover the lies told. When the lie or lies start unraveling people all over get hurt. They lose respect and trust toward that person. Trust is a hard thing to earn back. It takes a long time.

Walter Scott 1771-1832 gave a quote – "Oh, what a tangled web we weave, when first we practice to deceive."

When we deceive, we must remember what we told and to whom we told what. It becomes a web of lies and even the person can- not keep up with all that expands from one lie.

We can also get into deceptive thinking that what we do is ok, when it is not. We think we can break the rules and breaking them will not affect us or those around us. We think rules apply to others, but not to us. What a lie and self-deception. The laws of God have repercussions to all who break them. The grace of God may let things go okay for a time, but when that grace period is gone the repercussions will come. This is known as lawlessness.

There is so much lawlessness I see going on today. People think they are not only above the law of God, but above the laws of man. I see people parking where it says, "no parking". I guess people think it applies to everyone but them.

Ananias & Sapphira are perfect examples of this:

- Acts 5:1-11 - Now a man named Ananias, together with his wife Sapphira, also sold a piece of property. 2 With his wife's full knowledge he kept back part of the money for himself but brought the rest and put it at the apostles' feet. 3 Then Peter said, "Ananias, how is it that Satan has so filled your heart that you have lied to the Holy Spirit and have kept for yourself some of the money you received for the land? 4 Didn't it belong to you before it was sold? And after it was sold, wasn't the money at your disposal? What made you think of doing such a thing? You have not lied just to human beings but to God. 5 When Ananias heard this, he fell and died. And great fear seized all who heard what had happened. 6 Then some young men came forward, wrapped up his body, and carried him out and buried him. 7 About three hours later his wife came in, not knowing what had happened. 8 Peter asked her, "Tell me, is this the price you and Ananias got for the land?" "Yes," she said, "that is the price." 9 Peter said to her, "How could you conspire to test the Spirit of the Lord? Listen! The feet of the men who buried your husband are at the door, and they will carry you out also." 10 At that moment she fell down at his feet and died. Then the young men came in and, finding her dead, carried her out and buried her beside her husband. 11 Great fear seized the whole church and all who heard about these events.

God hates the sin of lying.

When a door is open to pride it is hard to help a person to see it. Pride can make us feel special and unique, so it is hard for a person to accept or see pride in themselves. I am not talking about the uniqueness of being a creation in Christ, but what makes us feel set above or more important than other members of the body of Christ, or other people. Pride causes us to concentrate on our rights and what we deserve instead of serving others. It does not think it is wrong. Pride can be in the form of self- pity. It can be in the form of lack of forgiveness, thinking we deserve the right to not forgive because of how unjustly we were hurt in a situation. It can make us think we are humble and not look at the idea we may have pride. What usually happens is people begin to see it in some- one, and our friends and those people once around us tend to not be in our lives anymore.

Pride wants not to be vulnerable to anyone. It builds walls around us, thinking we are protecting our self. It may say nobody will ever have my whole heart.

Pride can go the opposite direction and produces a fear of man.

We become more concerned with what people think than what God says or thinks. Pride produces an un-teachable spirit. Pride produces selfish interests over other's needs. Pride does not believe it is wrong. Have you ever thought yourself so right in being right, that you were wrong in how you handled or reacted to the situation?

If someone you know has pride, begin praying for God to break it down in that person's life. They do not need the destruction it brings in, even though they may experience some to see them freed.

It is always good for us to have someone we can go to and ask if they are picking up any pride on us. It will help us keep in check with ourselves.

- Proverbs 16:18 - Pride goes before destruction, a
  haughty spirit before a fall.

Idolatry

Idolatry is anything that is put above God or is not God. It can be distorting our priorities to God and our family. It can be doing something intentional or not intentional that puts something above God in our lives. It can be worshipping creation other than God.

Years ago, I knew a pastor's wife who went to an Asian country. She took a tour and was led down into the ground of a temple of worship for one of their deities. She came back to the USA and for 3 years after that trip, she was constantly sick. Doctors could not figure out what was wrong. She sought prayer every chance she could, for the sickness to be gone. Then one day the Lord showed her a vision of going down into the temple of worship that was on the tour. At one point she had to bow low to go into the temple area. She immediately knew what the Lord was saying and repented for bowing down to another god and idols that were in that temple. She was immediately healed.

There is only one God. Scripture is very precise about not having any other god or deity before Him.

- Exodus 20:3 - "You shall have no other gods before me."
- Exodus 34:14 - Do not worship any other god, for the Lord, whose name is Jealous, is a jealous God.

We all must make our own judgment calls in our lives. For me, I will not do Yoga or other things along those lines. I did not let my kids do karate. The reason for all this was because I did a study and a lot of the moves in Yoga and Karate are moves, they do, to worship the deities of their gods.

Yoga may look all innocent, and some even use Christian music and prayer with it. It has ungodly roots. Yoga is one of the six schools of Hindu philosophical traditions. The god called Kundalin is in its roots. The purpose was to unite (yoke with or join) with this higher power. Some Christians who practice yoga say they do not focus on its pagan religions; they focus on Jesus and chant Jesus. The problem is I can chant Jesus while I cast occult spells, it does not make it ok. It stills opens a door for the demonic.

I am careful what I bring into my home and go by my first instinct about something. I always pray over anything from other cultures, countries, and believe it or not, antiques. Things that are not of God can attach to these things and open a door. I want my home peaceful and a sanctuary for my family.

My friend Jean went to a Chiropractor. When she was there, she felt New Age all around in that practice. That night when she went to bed that doctor appeared to her and wanted to introduce her to a spirit guide. She is a well-known prophet, and the doctor must have picked up on her gifting. He did an out of the body projection. She said no you do not. In the name of Jesus, I command you out of here and I plead the blood of Jesus for protection. It left in a flash. She never went back there again.

I am so careful who I have do a massage for me. Careful what I linger around. If I am in a shop or place, I pick up negative feelings, I am out of there.

It is so important we know where we are and what is going on around us. Darkness uses the spiritual realm also. We must know what God is and what is not. Yes, God gives us His angels around us to protect us, but we must be wise and discern what is going on around us.

There was a restaurant I loved eating at. It had wonderful Latin food. It was doing great business wise. One day a friend and I went in. They had masks on the wall that were demonic looking. The owner's wife had gone to Mexico and brought the masks back to decorate. I talked to the owner saying I know you may not understand this, but you are going to lose a lot of customers from those masks. Within 6 months they were closed.

Chapter Nine

WHAT IS DELIVERANCE?

Some things will be revisited as I explain how deliverance can happen. Deliverance can come from a variety of ways and we will explore some of these. God can use anything he chooses to heal his people. Yes, deliverance is healing, it can be being set free from a negative energy or demonic hold, but it can also be emotional healing.

Deliverance through Healing

Deliverance in healing is being set free from something that keeps someone in bondage. It can be just forgiving someone. It can be someone understanding THEIR sin in a matter and simply asking God's forgiveness with being terribly sorry. Too many times we focus on the other person instead of focusing on our part of a problem and we wonder why things do not get healed. Healing can look like a team of people praying over someone and everything is calm. It can look like someone going bonkers with yelling and screaming as a group of people or a person lay hands on someone (this is rare, but it happens). It can be a simple understanding about what needs to change, and the heart is changed. It can be a lot of counseling and prayer, because just like an onion we may have layers to peel off. It can be a word from someone or from a minister teaching God's word. It can be by reading a book, or finally seeing or hearing truth about things.

People need deliverance or set free from past things in their lives or from generational things passed down so they can become all that God intended them to become and set their lives on a right path for the blessings of God.

Most people, when hearing the word deliverance, immediately get an image of a movie that came out in the 70's called "The Exorcist". There is a demon possessed girl having a deep dark voice and her head of a spinning around as Catholic priest does deliverance on her. Even though this was based on a true story, Hollywood put their twist on it. This type of deliverance has happened through the ages, but on rare occasions.

Deliverance through Understanding

- In John 8:32 states, "Then you will know the truth, and the truth will set you free."

Having an understanding in our heart and mind can be a type of deliverance. When we finally get it and no longer go into direction of sin. It is like a light bulb lights up in the darkness and we finally see and understand.

- In Revelation 12:11 it says "They overcame him because of the blood of the Lamb and by the word of their testimony" .... We all have a testimony to share because of Jesus shed His blood and we became over comers walking out of it in this side of life. Our testimonies can be used to set people free.

God knows who we are and the timing of us being set free and being restored. People can all be telling us the same thing, but sometimes someone comes, and it all makes sense. So never give up with someone. Does not mean you stay and be abused. I am talking about being a true friend and listening to God. Saying the same thing even if they do not seem to hear.

Deliverance through a Touch

Just a touch from Jesus to a person's heart can start a healing to set the captive free.

I remember being in Portland Oregon at the Clackamas Town Center when Jesus gave me a vision of myself getting married to a tall man and feeling wonderfully loved and covered. A marriage to a man I dearly loved had just ended. To me, when I made the covenant vow to my ex-husband in marriage, I was in it for life. Unfortunately, my husband at that time was not a healed man. I did not understand about sexual addictions and how much in bondage my husband was. He was in an orphanage at a young age and in between foster homes till he was 6 or so. He lived a double life through our marriage and when it came to being exposed, the divorce happened. I was getting a legal separation, but he wanted a divorce. This broke my heart, as when we married, I intended it to be till death do us part.

After having this vision, a healing began in my heart. One touch from God to my broken heart, was all it took for a healing to begin and hope to come forth regarding my future. In time God brought a wonderful tall man into my life and brought such restoration to my life. We married and I have never felt so loved, secure, and protected by someone. Jesus of course is the ultimate one, but my husband now is second to none! The Lord told me I would see a healed man compared to an un-healed man. That I did.

Deliverance through Forgiveness

Going to a person and humbly asking forgiveness for your part in a matter can bring deliverance and healing to a person or relationship. Unforgiveness keeps us tied in chains spiritually, to the person we will not forgive, and ties Gods hands to help us. It does not mean we put them back in our lives, or that they deserve it. It means we free our hearts and can move forward leaving God to deal with them and being set free from bitterness or what could have come on us holding on to a situation.

Even Jesus on the cross faced this dilemma with those who were murdering Him, He asked Father God to forgive them for they do not know what they are doing.

- Luke 23:34 Jesus said, "Father, forgive them, for they do not know what they are doing." And they divided up his clothes by casting lots.

Forgiveness is such a big key for deliverance. How can we ask God to forgive us if we still have not forgiven others in our life?

Deliverance through Worship and music

Worship in church or hearing a song can be healing and begin to set a person free. The song could be worship or secular (to some people's amazement). Songs open us up to His presence. He created music, even though the enemy uses it wrongly. Heaven is full of Worshiping God and Music. God can use it to soften our hearts and take the walls down our mortal minds have built around our hearts, thinking we are protecting ourselves.

A lot of my childhood was interrupted, and pieces missing. God is concerned about every part of us. He began healing those years with music from that era to bring me to a whole state. I wish I could give you an understanding of what I am meaning, because even I cannot explain it in my religious thinking from what I was taught. It was not dark music that takes people down the wrong path, but what He chose to bring sweet healing in my life of the years I missed. My teen years. I got to enjoy the years I missed. In our minds secular music is not of God. All I know is God used it.

When my children were growing up, we did not allow music

that did not give Glory to God. They listened to wonderful music by Christian rock bands and were fed spiritually. Would I still do it the same? Two of my children would have been fine with secular music and would not have been pulled into the dark music, but two would have been pulled in a wrong place. So, I probably would do the same, but understanding why, not thinking all music was wrong.

Another amazing time I remember going to sleep one night. All night this choir of angels sang to me a worship song from the 70's...Sing Hallelujah to the Lord...Sing Hallelujah to the Lord. Sing Hallelujah, Sing Hallelujah, Sing Hallelujah to the Lord.... Over and over all night. I even got up to go to the bathroom and when I got back into bed, it continued. I am not sure what was happening, but I remember a difference in whom I was. Healing happened as a choir of angel's sang over me through the night.

Deliverance through Uncommon Ways

God can use anything He chooses. In some instances, God even used handkerchiefs, aprons, the shadow of Peter, and a donkey.

- Act's 19:12 – God did extraordinary miracles through Paul. So that even handkerchiefs and aprons that had touched him (Paul) were placed on the sick, and their illnesses were cured, and the evil spirits left them.
- Acts 5:15 – People brought the sick into the streets and laid them on beds and mats so that at least Peter's shadow might fall across them as he went by. One thing we should note is that the Bible said "God did extraordinary miracles through Paul. Notice it was not Paul who did the miracles; it was God who did them.
- Numbers 22:28 – The Lord opened the donkey's mouth and the donkey said to Balaam, "What have I done to you to make you beat me these three times?" The

donkey having seen the angel holding a sword in the
road and did not want to go forward.

In 1996, I had a chance to go to St. Petersburg, Russia, with
some other pastors, evangelists, prophets and apostles. The
marriage with the ex at the time was not doing well. I was so
emotional and felt totally out of touch within myself of who I was,
or God was in me. We had gone to a church meeting in St. Petersburg with about 200 people. At the end, they wanted the Americans to pray for the people. I did not want to pray. I felt so not
"holy" enough. The people lined up in front of the Americans in
lines. When I started praying for people, the people standing in
front of me started falling out under the spirit. (This is when the
spirit of God comes on someone and they kind of faint and lie out
on the floor as the Holy Spirit starts healing them.) It shocked me.
Then people standing in other lines ran over and started lining up
where I was praying. All I know is that I wanted to run out of
there because I felt so unworthy. (My son whose wife is Russian,
and him being a missionary to Romania, told me that was an
unusual happening in Russia at that time).

A year later, I learned one of the people I had prayed for, had
been diagnosed with liver cancer. She was completely healed. The
doctors could not figure it out. What I learned is it was not me. I
was not worthy, but God who heals, is. It does not matter how I
feel, worthy or not. Miracles are about what He (The Lord)
decides to do. Not who I am or what I am going through. And not
by what or what not a person does. He can use any thing He
chooses for some one's healing, whether health wise or spiritually,
He wants to heal us. It is in His hands and timing. Not our
thinking or ways.

Deliverance through Inner Healing

Inner healing is another way deliverance can happen. We live in
a world of hurting human beings who hurt others. In the spiritual

realm there are many fallen angels whose assignment is to keep us unhealed, not fulfilling our destiny, and away from receiving Jesus in our hearts. It is so important to be set free with inner healing. Whether from tapes or books, we can begin deliverance and healing in our lives.

Many times, in our lives the enemy brings in hurts, trauma, destruction, and situations that alter who we are. Others who share their life through books, media, are giving their testimony. Hearing their testimony can set us in the path of healing and deliverance. By hearing or knowing the truth, we can be set free and healed.

- John 8:32 - 32 Then you will know the truth, and the truth will set you free."

Note: Please check out John L. Sandford's books and tapes at elijahhouse.org

Deliverance from God's Word

In 1985 when we were pastoring a church in Texas, I was following my husband and kids home. I got home and stepped out of the car and let out a blood curdling scream. I felt like someone had taken a knife and stabbed me in my neck. I felt something scampering down my shirt. I ran into the house, and it happened again. It felt again like a knife stabbed me in my right side. When I took my blouse off, there was a scorpion that fell off the blouse. I had been stung by a scorpion. Knowing they were poisonous I remember thinking to myself about the TV show "Sanford and Son", when Sanford grabbed his chest and says, "I'm coming home Elizabeth." At that moment I realized I was not afraid to die, and thought if this is it, then I am ready to go be with Jesus. When I got to the emergency room, they took their time to get me in, so realized I was not dying. They told me I would be sick for 2 days, sicker than I may have ever felt, but that I would be fine. They said to take an over-the-counter antihistamine medicine. I had 2 welts the size of oranges where I had been stung. They told me the black scorpions are the killers without antidote. When I got home that night my bible fell open to:

- Luke 10:19 – Behold, I have given you authority to tread on serpents and scorpions, and over all the power of the enemy, and nothing will injure you.

The next day I woke up and never had any sickness or swelling of any kind, from the stings of the scorpion. God had healed me with His Word. Not just the Bible but His word to me. His Word is another way He heals!

We must be careful of thinking if we do this or that I will be healed. Only if it truly is God directing.

When someone is healed in a certain way, we think that must be how to do it. NO. It is not about us, but about Him and what He does.

Sometimes there is an anointing that God may give to someone for a season, or we can be in a meeting and an anointing in the gathering happens. Again, it is Him. Not a man.

Deliverance through Physical or Emotional Healing

We can lay hands on others and ask God to come with His wonderful presence to see healing emotionally or physically. This is another way deliverance can happen.

- Mark 16:17-18 And these signs will accompany those who believe: In my name they will drive out demons; 18 they will pick up snakes with their hands; and when they drink deadly poison, it will not hurt them at all; they will place their hands-on sick people, and they will get well."

One thing we must remember the Lord knows what His timing is and what He is doing in this individual. If you do not see it at that moment, does not mean He is not answering the prayer or healing that person. Every time I lay hands on a person, I trust Him to do what He desires and knows to do. People can have layers that need peeled back slowly. Do not over think things, God is in control of it all and each individual healing and time of healing!

One thing I have seen is when people pray and someone does not get healed, then they think it is because the person does not want healed. Do not get into that line of thinking. God is God and He sets the timing, and He knows what needs done first. Maybe He is doing other things in that person's life.

- Matthew 6:25-34 Therefore I tell you, do not be anxious about your life, what you will eat or what you will drink, nor about your body, what you will put on. Is not life more than food, and the body more than clothing? Look at the birds of the air: they neither sow nor reap nor gather into barns, and yet your heavenly Father feeds them. Are you not of more value than they? And which of you by being anxious can add a single hour to his span of life? And why are you anxious for clothing? Consider the lilies of the field, how they grow: they neither toil nor spin, yet I tell you, even Solomon in all his glory was not arrayed like one of these.

God is in control of it all.

The Timing of Deliverance

Deliverance or healing can happen all at once or can take time with layer after layer. It can be like peeling away each layer of an onion. Jesus can give us an instantaneous healing, but usually it does not happen that way. My thinking is that He wants us to be a testimony with walking things out, so we can be a help to others. But if it is instantaneous, praise God!!! Never think God forgets anyone. We need to trust God and His timing. We need to encourage those, who think God has overlooked them. He has not. He knows what He is doing. He takes each of us individual and nobody fits in the same box.

Deliverance of Demons with a Stronger Hold Over Someone

We held a lot of Bible studies in our home through the years. We were leading a study in the early 80's and an individual came to receive prayer. Our children were in grade school and sleeping, as it was about 9:30 at night. When we started praying, a peculiar phenomenon started happening. What looked like a small round looking tumor started rolling under this man's skin. We would pray and it would run under the skin to another part of his limbs, and his chest. We would apply prayer to that area, and it would move to another area on his body. After about 45 minutes, the man let out a big scream, peace came on him, and the ball under his skin was gone. My children, who were in bed, heard the scream and still remember that night. It was demonic and this person was set free. His whole life turned around. We were sure to pray over our home as we did not want anything to try to harm our children.

It is important to know that when ministering to a person we must treat them with the love and compassion of Jesus. Whether they have demonic holds, or the demons present themselves, there is still a suffering person in that body. Our yelling and screaming does not manifest more anointing. It is God who anoints for deliverance, not the way the person is praying. We must keep our eyes and worship off man and only onto God.

We can read many books on demonology and deliverance but know this; demons do not go by the books you may have read. It is important to listen to the Holy Spirit when we pray for anyone, for deliverance and everything in our lives. There is nothing new

under the sun (Ecclesiastics), but the demons have practiced from
the time they were put out of Heaven, how to trick and use things.

- Ecclesiastes 1:9 – What has been, will be again, what has
  been done will be done again; there is nothing new
  under the sun.

Unless the Holy Spirit tells you to, do not communicate with a
demon or ask questions. They are liars. You cannot believe them.
Do not believe what is said. The demons will also try to bring fear
into the people praying. Do not come into fear. The demonic feeds
and strengthen their self through fear, hate, jealousy and emotions.

Things to Help in Deliverance

There are different levels of demonic activity. Some are easily
overcome, and others are not. Sometimes demons may have some
extraordinarily strong holds in the person. There can be more than
one demonic power tied to another. Getting to a root of why the
demons are there and how they are working together, can help to
see layers loosed. So, do not be dismayed if everything is not taken
care of in one session of deliverance. It is important for the person
to repent of sins and involvement in things not of God. We must
listen as the Holy Spirit may bring things up that need repenting
from either the person praying or to the individual that is getting
prayer. Just remember there are many ways things can come to us
in praying for a person and the one being delivered. Asking questions of the person seeking deliverance may help for direction. We
need to be discerning if our feelings are from the Holy Spirit or
are, we just picking up their feelings or what their heart wants.
People who are sensitive can even pick-up other people's "stuff" or
"feelings", from those who are praying with you. You could be
hearing a demonic subconscious voice, or our own hearts. Or we
will be hearing the Holy Spirit and that is what we want. It is so
important to be a gentleman just as the Holy Spirit is. We need to

be sensitive not only of the person we are praying for, but sensitive to those who are praying with us. Be considerate and not think you are the most important person there. God cannot work through our pride or arrogance.

I always ask if what I am hearing makes sense to them. Letting them know I miss it sometimes. If it does not, then I ask permission to pray it anyway, just to make sure we cover all that we can. People are very receptive to this and they do not become wounded. We want to be as gentle as a dove but wise as a serpent and not bring more hurts to a person.

Permission for Deliverance

Before prayer or deliverance, it is important to have permission and know if truly a person wants prayer and deliverance. Luke 11:26 and Matthew 12:43-45 talks about a person being delivered, but the demon goes and finds 7 more wicked spirits and they enter him. That is why, if we see a demon in a person, we do not think it is our job to do deliverance, unless God says to. I will not do deliverance unless it manifests in front of me AND OR God says to do so.

- Luke 11: 24 "When an impure spirit comes out of a person, it goes through arid places seeking rest and does not find it. Then it says, 'I will return to the house I left.' 25 When it arrives, it finds the house swept clean and put in order. 26 Then it goes and takes seven other spirits more wicked than itself, and they go in and live there. And the final condition of that person is worse than the first."
- Matthew 12:43 "When an impure spirit comes out of a person, it goes through arid places seeking rest and does not find it. 44 Then it says, 'I will return to the house I left.' When it arrives, it finds the house unoccupied, swept clean and put in order. 45 Then it goes and takes

with it seven other spirits more wicked than itself, and
they go in and live there. And the final condition of that
person is worse than the first. That is how it will be
with this wicked generation."

Always ask the person for their permission to pray for them. So
important! Sometimes though manifestations my happen and that
may be impossible to do. If this happens God is allowing this, and
you need to go in and listen to the Holy Spirit and see this person
set free.

Recently my daughter-in-law was praying over a child for healing. A word of knowledge came to her that the mother did not
want the child healed. As they asked the mother if that was true,
she said yes, because that was how her income was coming in,
through her child's disabilities. Sad, but there are reasons sometimes God cannot do what it is we are praying for. And then sometimes it is because He knows what is best for a person's process of
becoming more like Christ. Lack of healing or deliverance does
not always mean someone is bad or at fault. The question was
asked, "Who sinned, has man or his parents. The answer was
neither."

- John 9:2-3 – His disciples asked him, "Rabbi, who
  sinned, this man or his parents, that he was born blind?"
  3 "Neither this man nor his parents sinned," said Jesus...

We have a special person in our family who is in their 20's and
has a disease that is rare and needs a kidney transplant. He
received Christ in his heart and was in a group that believed he
would be healed. My understanding is that when he was not healed
like the group felt he should, they told him he was at fault because
his faith was not there. Because of this he says he is not a Christian
anymore. I would not want to be the ones standing before Christ
who conveyed this to him. There are again many reasons why
healing does not happen. God may have a better way than an

instantaneous healing. What if he goes through the transplant and God uses doctors and medicine to bring this man to health? Then this man can be a testimony for others who will go through the same situation. God says that our faith needs to be as a mustard seed.

- Matthew 17: 20 He replied, "Because you have so little faith. Truly I tell you, if you have faith as small as a mustard seed, you can say to this mountain, 'Move from here to there,' and it will move. Nothing will be impossible for you."

A mustard seed is the smallest seed. You hardly can see it. For me He is saying that it has nothing to do with our faith, for it can be tiny. What it has to do with is our belief that He is who He is. It is not about us.

My ex-husband ended up in the hospital in ICU with Pancreatitis. He almost died twice. They gave him little chance of surviving. I finally concluded to trust God in the situation whether He healed my ex-husband or not. It was when I gave it to God and extensively trusted Him no matter the outcome, God started the healing. In 3 days, my husband walked the hospital hall in ICU. The doctors, nurses, and all stood in a line and clapped joyously. They called him the miracle man. It was all because of who God is, not how much faith I had or did not have.

What if someone is not healed on this side of the spectrum but is healed on the other side, in Heaven. It all is healing. We need to view things from God's perspective and not our own limited understanding of things. Do not put God in a box. He can do whatever He feels is right for that person.

Exposure

God is always into restoration. As children we always hated discipline, but as parents we understand it is needed. God is into discipline, because of the love for His children. Pastoring I have watched God give a grace period before the disciplining.

I have seen two Pastor's fall. There has always been the grace period given. One was at a church where we attended. And the other I knew well.

In the first incident we had gone to East Texas to pioneer a church. The pastor's wife called me and started confiding in me about how strange her husband was becoming. She could not say much to anyone in the church. As time went on his behavior became more irrational. I cannot remember why I ended going there, but I went. While there we prayed a lot and in one of the prayer times, I heard a strange thing. I heard the pastor was seeing one of the Elder's daughters. To me, I thought I was crazy to think that, but I confronted the pastor with it. It turned out what I heard was right. Of course, the pastor fled. Unfortunately, that was not God's heart. He wanted truth to come out so the pastor could get help and be restored. That is always the heart of God. The church needs to understand restoration more than it does. They have a long way to learn the heart of God in restoring people.

Wisdom is so important when someone is pastoring. The other pastor had issues from childhood that he never got help with. He was abandoned at age 3 and was in orphanages and foster homes. He had been disciplined once for having an emotional relationship with another woman in the body. After his discipline was done, he ended up pastoring a church. The presence of the God was thick in the church. My son led worship and people began being healed and restored. Unfortunately, unless healing happens there is a door left open. Thinking the last incident was behind, no one understood what would come. The enemy was not happy with what was happening in the church. The enemy hates seeing God heal and restore. The pastor began counseling women alone. Many tried to speak wisdom to him about not doing this. He thought he was beyond the wisdom of the Elders and what others tried to convey. People who came into the church to minister started seeing a lot of pride in this man. He did not believe it. As time went on, he would continue meeting and counseling women alone. Women came and would report of his flirtatious ways. Several single women left the church. When the wife went to Russia on a mission trip, the teenage children went to the Elders, as he was spending hours in the evenings and nights not home.

No one knew what was going on. The Elders and the Ministers called in suggested to hire a detective. When they hired the detective, they did not know it was someone he had went to college with years before. She did not know him, but he knew her because she was the president of the body when he had been there. He had caught her sitting out watching the church. He went and invited her in. She was trying to stay incognito so decided to go in. When she came into his office, he tried to take advantage of her. He did admit to this to his wife and minister when confronted with the detective. He was asked to step down and get healing for a season. He would not accept this. He told his wife no church, no marriage. Sad. God exposed it, to see restoration for him. Unfortunately, he did not walk it out at that time in his life.

Other Things to Consider

In a church or ministry setting, it would be wise to have a team trained to minister deliverance.

Training a team that can flow together and have different gifts of the Holy Spirit will make a safer situation for the person that is receiving prayer and deliverance. Our hope and goal should be that people being ministered to are not wounded more than before we met them, and those praying have accountability in a set up prayer situation.

I suggest, before a scheduled prayer or deliverance, the person being prayed for do a check up with a doctor for blood work and making sure there is nothing physically going on. Our body is so intricately made, one thing can be off and what we think is a spiritual problem may end up being a physical – health problem. After working with doctors for years I know a blood work up can tell a lot. There is so much wisdom in this. Not everything is demonic and knowing what an issue is can help us solve the problem faster through prayer and help medically, as needed. It will also give us a correct target to hit for our prayers.

For those on a prayer team, having a pregnant woman on a prayer team is not wise. If a demonic presence shows up, it could cause physical harm and there can be a danger of transference of a spirit to the child in the womb. Please heed this warning!

Because of a transference that can happen to you, it is good to ask the Lord if you are to lay hands on someone. Listen to the Holy Spirit, He will guide and protect you. I am very aware and do not like just anybody laying hands on me. Going into any situation I will cover myself and others with the Blood of Jesus.

I find it interesting that in Mark 5:12 the demons begged Jesus, "Send us among the pigs; allow us to go into them." Jesus allowed this. It shows me that animals can be possessed by demons, too. So, if deliverance is taking place of a home with animals pray protection for them.

Always best to pray for someone's deliverance in the daylight hours. Sometimes this may not work out this way if a demonic hold makes itself present. The reason why is that darkness gives the demonic realm more power. It hates light. For some reason, the time between midnight and 3 a.m. is known as the witching hour. Just be wise in all things.

Be Led by the Holy Spirit

In the mid 80's, a well-known deliverance minister came to the church we pastored in East Texas. He shared a story about a deliverance he was involved in. He told the story about one day when a knock came to his door. He opened the door and there was a group of people there looking all worn out. Some had torn clothing and looked like they had just been in a fight. He invited them in, and they told their story about someone they knew well, whom they had tried to do deliverance on. As they told the story, they talked about how she would run on the walls and ceiling in superhuman speed, and how the place looked like a tornado had hit it. Wisely, he told them that he would pray and if God said to, he would come. They left. He prayed and felt he was to go. When he got there, he saw the house did look like a tornado had hit it and the group of people, were there. He sat down at the table and started reading his Bible. All the sudden the girl started running up the walls and on the ceiling in superhuman speed. He heard the Lord say, "When she faces you, face to face, perpendicular on the wall, then cast the demon out." Her running everywhere went on for a while with him just sitting at the table calmly. The people with her were getting agitated by his just sitting there. Then all the sudden she was facing him perpendicular on the wall and he heard the Lord say, "Now". He cast the demon out and the girl was set free immediately.

There is so much to learn from this. He showed wisdom, patience, and was obedient to God. He did not give in to all the chaos going on around him. He did not fear. He knew the spiritual realm is real and all around us. There was no pride. He knew who God is.

Sometimes we become "hyper-spiritual" and think everything is spiritual or demonic. We can be so spiritually high that we are no earthly good. We end up not relating to those around us. This is a religious spirit. God created both the heavenly realm and the earth. He wants us to function on both planes in balance!

I have no problem with people getting books to help them understand or seeking wisdom from other ministries. What I do have a problem with is people seeking prophecies from wherever they can run to get one or trying to find someone who agrees with their thinking on things. We can all hear God ourselves, if we will listen. People hear what they want to hear.

They run here and there for a word from someone. They trust all the teachings they hear and do not balance it out with the Bible and use one scripture to prove what they want to believe.

- 2 Timothy 4:3- 3 For the time will come when people will
  not put up with sound doctrine. Instead, to suit their
  own desires, they will gather around them a great
  number of teachers to say what their itching ears want
  to hear.

There is a teaching that came about in biblical times called
Manichaeism. It was named after a religious figure named Mani
and was taught as heresy in the early church. Manichaeism is an
extreme form of dualistic Gnosticism. It promises salvation
through the attainment of special knowledge of spiritual truths. It
also argues that the foundation of the universe is the opposition of
two principles, good and evil, each equal in relative power. Knowledge becomes puffed up and then becomes not teachable. Knowledge is not a bad thing, but it is not the answer. The Pharisees and
Sadducees were a good example of this. They felt they had knowledge and knew the OT scriptures backward and forwards. They
would walk around looking holy and let everyone know if they
were fasting and so forth. They were puffed up and were religious
without a relationship with God. God sent His son and they
missed it and persecuted the Messiah they believed would come.

Religion does this to us. Man tells us we must do this and that
to be holy and saved. Or this and that so God will hear us or heal
us. We cannot attain any salvation for what we do or do not do or
what we know or do not know. It is because of Christ giving his life
at the cross for our sins and asking Him into our hearts and life. It
is a gift that has been given.

What we forget is that Christ said it is finished and the enemy
was defeated at the cross.

Many Christians walk on the side of the cross thinking we still
have this huge battle to fight. Yes, battles still happen but it has
been finished! We only need to battle when Christ calls us into
battle. We do not need to take on battles that are not ours to fight.
So many Christians have been worn out doing spiritual warfare
that they are not called to do. Everybody has a unique walk of

their own. That is how Christ made it. We need to find how He wants us to walk with Him and not think we are called as others may be called. Stay out of things that you are not called to and ask Him what He wants.

There was a pastor I knew well. He decided to in prayer to go after a demonic principality in the heavens. We were all in a prayer group. When he started, I thought no, no. We were not called to fight that principality. I started covering the people with the blood of Christ. The pastor fell to the ground, got sick and could not get up. He learned that night not to mess where he is not called.

Healing in Communion

Communion is a common place God heals. When we take communion properly, meaning with true repentance in our hearts, He can heal. It is His son's blood and His forgiveness to us. Nothing is more powerful than that.

I remember going to church and my throat being so sore. I was always susceptible to strep throat. I remember thinking I so do not need being sick as I had three young children at home. I remember drinking the grape juice down my throat and it was burning intensely. Just like that no pain. To this day I have never had strep throat. When he heals, he totally heals!

When Something Really Is Not Demonic

There are a few things I want to share. The reason for this is to understand how careful we need to be calling things demonic when we are not sure what is what.

When pastoring a church in Oregon a pentagram was done in chalk outside the church doors. Because of the presence of God in the services, we knew we were making the enemy mad. People were being set free and healed. Many well know ministers came through to preach and told us there was such a presence of God there. In fact, the presence would be so thick it looked like a mist throughout the sanctuary. One day the phone rang and a voice that was deep and growling like a demon and a deep demonic voice telling me how it wanted to harm us. I quickly hung up the phone in shock. I immediately started praying in the spirit. The phone rang immediately again. I picked it up and the same voice said for me to stop praying that way. Was it someone possessed or was it a demon? I will never know.

I am sharing this because often we give the demonic more power in our lives than it should have.

We become afraid and fear increases their power. Or we over think just what has happened, and again giving to much recognition.

I knew enough not to dwell on it and give anything power undeserved. You see, the battle has already been won. It is just walking it out with Christ leading us.

I remember waking up the next morning after that incident and a huge gardener snake was curled up under the end table next to the couch, the very next morning. Was that just coincidence? I do not know, but again I was not going to give it power that it did not deserve. I prayed over the house and went on with my life. My God is bigger!

Just recently we were vacationing in our 27-foot trailer. At 3:00 a.m. the light on the entertainment device kept flashing on and off till morning. Some people would immediately think it would be demonic because of the time it was doing it. I did not feel it was demonic and my husband read the manual and hit a reset button. The light has not flickered on and off since.

On this vacation a storm hit the area with heavy rain and gust of winds up to 65 mph. I shared this on social media. Some people's responses were interesting. Some rebuked the winds and rain in the name of Jesus. Not judging them because they are doing what religion has taught them. What we need to understand is that God allows winds and storms. Even in our lives to change us into being more like Him. If God tells us to rebuke the winds, then yes, we need to do it, but not on our own thinking. We need balance with our walk in Christ so unbelievers will be attracted to the gospel, not turned off by our behaviors, or silliness. And yes, I understand that sometimes Christ does tell us to do things that are not status quo.

Silly Things

My present husband, before I met him, was attending a church and God told him to stand on his head and prophesy to a congregation. He thought, "What". He did it in obedience to Christ. Miracles happened and people repented.

In the Bible God used Peter's shadow, Acts 5:14 to 16. God used Paul's apron and handkerchief, acts 19: 11, 12. He used Elijah's mantle, 2 Kings 2:9 – 14. And much more. Each thing that has happened in our lives, God knew, before we were born. What will get us through the times ahead is, trusting the Lord and obeying Him.

- In 1Samuel 15:22-23 it says –Obedience is better than sacrifice, and submission is better than offering the fat of rams. Rebellion is as sinful as witchcraft and stubbornness as bad as worshiping idols.

Conclusion

From the beginning of this earth, the spiritual realm is the spiritual realm. God created it all. It always is with us. We cannot always see it, and many will never experience the things others have experienced. That does not mean one person is better than another, nor does it mean the spiritual realm does not exist. It does mean we need to live our lives, be aware of the devices of the enemy, but not look for demons everywhere. God created balance and wants us to walk in His balance of things. With all I have shared I just want others to be aware of what is and how we can open doors we are unaware of. Only you can walk your walk with

God. He loves you and wants the best for you as your Father. He wants us free and whole as we walk this life. We know for sure will be free and whole in Heaven with Him.

The Bible says in James 4:7 – Resist the devil and he will flee.

In these days we need to be wise as a serpent and as gentle as a dove. We need to know what we are facing and not fearing the unknown. Balance in all things always. A wise Pastor pounded this into us... Roy Hicks, Jr.

Many people could add more to this and go in deeper with what they have been taught, but I wanted this to be applicable to everyone who is living in this day and time and wake up those who have never considered these things. Anyone can do further study into this. All I know is Father you are the Alpha and Omega, the beginning and the end. In you I trust.

ABOUT THE AUTHOR

Pamela Squire has pastored two churches starting in the 1980s through 1996. She also worked as a Certified Medical Assistant and triaged for eight doctors until she retired in 2010.

Pamela has four adult children and 17 grandchildren. She has a heart for restoration and seeing God's people become all that He created them to be.